WOMEN AND ART

WOMEN AND CRAFT

Edited by
GILLIAN ELINOR
SU RICHARDSON
SUE SCOTT
ANGHARAD THOMAS
KATE WALKER

Published by VIRAGO PRESS Limited 1987
41 William IV Street, London WC2N 4DB

Copyright this collection © Gillian Elinor,
Su Richardson, Sue Scott, Angharad Thomas, Kate Walker 1987

Text design by Jo Laws
British Library Cataloguing in Publication Data
Women and craft.
  1. Handicraft
  I. Elinor, Gillian
  745.5   TT145

ISBN 0-86068-540-3

Typeset by Rowland Phototypesetting Ltd
Bury St Edmunds, Suffolk
Printed in Great Britain by
Anchor Brendon Ltd, Tiptree, Essex

Back jacket photography by:
top left: David Roberts, bottom left: Mary-Jo Major,
right: Anni Silverleaf.

CONTENTS

ACKNOWLEDGEMENTS

We thank all of the women who have written to us during the compilation of this book, together with all who have given their time to be interviewed. We should especially like to thank our families and friends for their support and, in particular, Solveig Jorgensen, Monica Ross, Jonathan and Sas, Ben, Bridget, Cindy, Hannah, Mick, Steve, Vicky, Vi and Walter.

PREFACE

To document the craftworking lives of women from a feminist point of view means looking at the things women make in terms of the women who make them. It does not mean seeing objects in isolation, the way art is often viewed; nor describing technique alone, which is how craft can be dismissed from view. But it does mean a perspective on the woman and her work within her social environment. There is a world of difference between the slopwork of the hard-pressed homeworker, the thriftily darned bed-linen of the proud housewife and the embroidered anti-macassar of the yet more leisured woman. In exploring these differences we have attempted to reveal the conditions of the practice of women's craftwork.

This book is an outcome of the *Feminist Arts News* 1981 'Craft' issue, which raised some of the questions dealt with here: the relative status of crafts and arts, and the contrast between unpaid work for love and the highly priced professional artefact. For many years fine art interests have been absorbing crafts which were once women's by tradition. Some crafts have achieved a limited status as 'fine art'. This acceptance has been gained at the risk of reduction and containment of meaning – so that, for example, a quilt may be analysed solely in terms of its abstract, formal qualities. The work is thus reduced to less than its actual meaning in the lives of its creators who made beautiful objects for the vital purpose of survival. On the road to re-evaluation, women's craftwork stands in danger of having its subtlety of meaning crushed by the powerful systems trading in fine art.

It is necessary to look beyond dominant values to the world of women's work. Here there is a submerged value-level, derived from women's assigned status as 'other' than artist – as housewife, mother and survivor. It is this other value system of which our contributors speak, almost half of whom, working with textiles, reflect still the domestic location of most women's craftwork. Women are the custodians of family history, they write about re-cycled materials, of cast-off clothes in rag rugs, of the elderly print frock in the patchwork. To take these values into the market of the male mode of cultural relations is to encounter problems of class as well as gender. Yet despite lack of recognition, low status, hard graft and minimal returns, many women have chosen their craft as a way of life and, variously, they celebrate it here.

This book celebrates the enduring capacity of craftswomen for turning the work of subsistence into the art of survival.

PART ONE

LABOUR OF LOVE

DOMESTIC CRAFTWORK

Jenny Larvin and Sue Pooley

OUR FAMILY HERITAGE
A conversation between two sisters

In this conversation between two sisters about
their family heritage of domestic craftwork, we find
how women communicate through craft activities,
how relationships are developed and transformed
through their work at home with each other.
These sisters spent their childhood in Birmingham;
Sue Pooley is still there. Jenny has moved from
Birmingham to Liverpool where she lives with two
of her children, aged nine and five. She works on a city
farm where she spins and dyes natural yarns.

In our family there are three generations of women
exercising a variety of craft skills. In our childhood we were unknowingly
influenced by the beauty of the things the older women made; we were
encouraged by them, given our rudimentary skills and warmed by the
affection expressed in the things they made for us. Now we may return
some of the support they gave to us.

Jenny: *'bone needles...'*
When I was seven or thereabouts I had been left at my grandmother's
and, being at a loss as to know what to do with me, she taught me to
knit. She sat in a high, hard chair by an old black range and I sat on a shoe
box by her side. From a deep bag containing hundreds or, to my child's
eye, millions of knitting 'pins' (as she always called them), she selected for
me a short pair of bone pins and said, 'These will do for you.' She put on
ten stitches and showed me the mechanics of the operation. She must
have had at least two hundred stitches on her needle since she was knitting
a fine, grey, ribbed skirt, and at the end of each of her rows she stopped
to check how I was managing my ten. Our knitting grew apace.

Sue: *'we'll buy some thread...'*
One of my most vivid recollections this – the first time I was away from
home, staying with my grandmother. I was about ten and feeling homesick
in a strange place with only her familiar face to comfort me, and so she

Nana Tipping
(b. 1894)
knitting
rag rugs
embroidery

Auntie Grace
(b. 1923)
sewing

Auntie Thelma
knitting
sewing

Father – Mother
(b. 1917)
sewing
painting
embroidery
writing
tapestry

Auntie Renee
(b. 1918)
embroidery

Jenny
(b. 1944)
crochet
knitting
sewing
embroidery
pottery
canalboat painting

Sue
(b. 1956)
sewing
macrame
embroidery
pottery
needlepoint

bought me some linen and silks and started to teach me to embroider. I was to make a dressing-table set to take home with me – a daunting task for such a novice. She seemed a stern, stiff woman to me then, but she worked very lovingly with me, giving me pride in the work and pleasure in the anticipated reception of it. I remember coming home bursting with the wonder of it because I had made it myself and could give it as a surprise. Of all the things I have made since, this is probably the most enduring and carefully looked after. My mother has it still.

Jenny: 'get a hook and I'll show you...'
Rag rugs were always part of our childhood home and recently I asked Nana how they had been made. She couldn't tell me beyond the fact that she used sugar sacks, and told me to get a hook and she would show me. In her youth the only soft floor coverings had been rag rugs and she continued to make them for her children's families long after they were necessary. I remember lying on a rug, sorting through rags and recognising pieces of my father's trousers, her old coats and bits of bright red ex-ambulance blankets. I never did make a rug, and probably since my craft skills have become less 'home-spun', I never will.

Sue: 'I'll make you one like it...'
With most things my mother made and still makes, one of the primary motives was to express her individuality. She never made a dress for herself without embroidering the collars, cuffs and pockets. The designs were always of her own making – I never saw a transfer used – and usually it was done in bright, contrasting colours. In answer to my envious cries she would always 'make me one like it'. I learned not to be entirely satisfied with wearing anything unless I had made some sort of personal mark upon it. Clothes were, and still are, an important means for me of expressing my personality, and I didn't ever feel comfortable merely 'following the fashion'.

Jenny: 'I like it to look real...'
Auntie Renee's house was very different from ours since she had no children. Everything was clean and precise, and somehow unapproachable. Every cushion was fat and exact, every chair covered in the places which would have worn had there been children to wear them. However, all the cushions and covers were most exquisitely embroidered. Not with the commonplace 'crinoline ladies' worked in backstitch outlines, but with elegant sheaves of corn, vines hung with grapes, grasses, poppies, all three-dimensional in their subtle shadings. She made tray-cloths, an unheard-of commodity at home, with real anemones gleaming with satin-stitched brilliance. With her I learned to embroider. Patiently, with small transferred samplers of cloth, she taught me, 'The back must always look as good as the front.' Today I smock my daughter's dresses and look guiltily at the unfinished tablecloths!

Sue: *'help me wind the wool...'*
My grandmother would arrive every Sunday morning bearing a bread pudding, and together with my mother and myself would prepare the meal. In the long, warm, cosy afternoons following, my father would sleep, and we would settle down together to talk and drink tea, always with some 'work' in hand. My grandmother produced endless streams of clothes on her knitting pins for all the family, from dolls' clothes to women's suits, and as she bought the yarn in hanks it fell to me to help her wind it off into manageable balls. Arms rigid, thumbs hooking the wool on my hands, it used to seem that the wool was never-ending, and all the time she nimbly wound, producing ball after perfect ball. The memory of those aching arms hasn't ever left me and I sometimes wonder if that's why I never did take to knitting myself!

'I've saved you some silks...'
The learning of these craft skills during childhood took place over a long period and was obviously very informally 'taught'. The supply of materials was always very uncertain – it was a question of using what you could get hold of, more often than not. My mother would buy me sixpenny bags of remnant pieces from the local dressmaker, teaching me along the way about the different textures and colours of fabrics, and what was best used for which article. My aunt, whom we visited regularly as she was housebound, would go to her cupboards and give me a bag of oddments of threads and silks. She made wonderful cakes for our visits, but I remember always feeling more anxious about the silks than the cakes until I got them. Nana, in her untiring efforts to make a knitter of me, saved her wool oddments, and Auntie Grace was a wonderful source of fancy trimmings. So, while we were a large family and acutely aware that money was scarce, we didn't lack stimulation, even if it wasn't in the form of the sophisticated, much coveted, shop-bought amusements!

Jenny: *'We'll see your Auntie Grace about that...'*
Every Christmas (and probably between times too, though I don't recall), I had a new dress made by my Auntie Grace. These were well made and 'sensible' with deep hems for letting down as I grew. They were good dresses but plain, even severe, so my mother would relieve them with embroidery in her usual way. I remember the blue dress with my initial on the collar, and a red one with flowers worked around the buttonholes. Because of her competence (and confidence), Auntie Grace acquired the perhaps doubtful honour of being the family dressmaker, and when we grew up she became the wedding-dress maker too. Every girl born into (not married into) the family has had her own and her bridesmaids' dresses made by this aunt, who was always very obliging about styles, fabrics and fancy nonsense such as fur, trains and pointed sleeves. From her I learned a delight in the use of beautiful and unusual buttons which, alas, are not readily available today, though jumble sales are often a good source.

*Sue's Punch, Judy and
Policeman glove puppets,
and below, Bargello
florentine wool embroidery
on canvas*

SUE POOLEY

Sue: Of all the bits and pieces that go to make up this patchwork of memory, the most clear are those connected with my mother. Being the last child, I fell less under the influence of aunts and grandmother than Jenny did. I felt as though I was on the border of another age: 'they' were all in the spider's web but I was only held to them by a tenuous line – that line, my mother. She never ceased to be my inspiration. The cry, 'I'm bored – what can I do?', which must have haunted her, was always met with a new idea, something different to make. Pleasure, entertainment and satisfaction were all to be found by actively expressing yourself through learned skills, and this way of looking at life has moulded the way I feel today. Now there are never enough hours in a day nor weeks in a month to achieve all I unrealistically look forward to. The cupboards are full of many half-finished projects – there is always something new that I'm itching to try out. In this way I feel that I've become a more self-reliant person; to be pleasurable, an activity has to be truly absorbing, and in some way creative.

To go back to the utility of articles made, on reflection this was probably the biggest spur when I was trying to master these skills as a child. Needlework, corking [French knitting] on wooden cotton reels, embroidery, were all learned as a means to an end, usually because I wanted to give one of the family a present. Birthday and Christmas gifts were, without exception, hand-made – this at a time when I had no money of my own. As I grew older I became more selective: only the favoured would receive a home-made present. This now seems quite remarkable to me, because I remember how impressed I was with the 'buying power' of money, and yet I chose to 'make'. Corking was a family addiction and as children we were positively competitive – we would work at it furiously, and furtively stretch it, each trying to make our own 'as long as the back garden'. Making things was fun, and later when we turned the woollen sausages into little table-mats there was real pride in the finished article.

Jenny: As for myself, I find that everything I do has its origins, in some way, in my childhood. I learnt patience and the pursuit of excellence, many techniques, a joy in beauty, in symmetry and individuality. I learnt to look at things in order to reproduce them and I learnt the pleasure to be had from giving. For these things I am immensely grateful, though all the women would be embarrassed by thanks, thinking that what they gave me was no more than part of a day's work.

The older women of the family have not only provided materials and expertise, but supported our efforts and valued the end products. We find that now we are adults the roles have been reversed to some extent. Our opinion is sought and respected, we are called upon for emotional support and confirmation in their endeavours. We have been able to teach them new techniques and encourage experimentation in different craft areas. Even on a practical level we are now often the providers of materials and ideas since age and illness have restricted their independence of movement.

We are aware that while these activities are constant there are definite peaks and troughs, the most productive times seeming to coincide with periods of emotional disturbance or physical incapacity. The only thing our grandmother doggedly persevered with, following a stroke, was her knitting. During Jenny's divorce we found that we had closed ranks with our mother in a tight support group, offering therapy in the form of an intense and prolonged period of making things for each other. During the worst three months, it seems to us now that by contriving this close triangle and sharing our handiwork, we were instinctively coming to terms with our own parts in the drama that was going on around us. Much talk, of course, went on at these times, but there seemed to be some powerful relationship between what we were doing with our hands, and the healing of our emotional wounds. This notion of 'craft as therapy' can be no more graphically demonstrated than in the case of our mother and her sister who are both severely crippled by muscular and wasting diseases. Unfortunately our aunt is now blind and can no longer practise her skill, but during the years of progressing disease she compensated for it by developing simple embroidery techniques. She used several shades of each colour placed in such a way that the images created a glowing three-dimensional art form. Our mother's illness has determined the skills she uses. When she was young her energies were used in painting large, dramatic canvases; when arthritis attacked her shoulders and wrists the paintings became small and delicate. Her need to express herself visually has led her into the use of needle skills, so now her canvases are small, and executed in wool instead of paint. It is interesting here to pick up the point that while she sees herself primarily as a creative artist, she is compelled to justify the time spent by making the 'art' functional, and so turns the tapestries into bags, purses and needle-cases. This compulsion seems to have been inherited by us, since the things we make also have to have a practical use.

Caroline and Margaret Blount

INFINITE TAKING OF PAINS
The 'sides-to-middle' world of women

The traditional 'sides to middle' world of women could set an oppressive standard of femininity, as Margaret Blount wryly syggests when she quotes her father's comment, 'You have an infinite capacity for taking pains.' Here, Caroline Blount interviews her mother Margaret, who now lives with her retired husband in a Suffolk village. Margaret's painstaking continues; she is currently completing a hexagonal, stuffed, patchwork quilt that Caroline began when she was sixteen. Caroline is now working towards setting up a community arts centre in Bradford.

C.: What is the first piece of craftwork that you remember doing?

M.: I was about four and I made a grey doll's scarf. It had edges that wiggled in and out and was about six inches long. I'd wanted to learn because I'd seen my grandmother knitting and I thought all she did was slip a stitch from one needle to the next – I wanted to know how it grew if that was all she was doing. She taught me how to knit. Before I was ten I had learnt how to turn the heel of a sock, although mother hadn't been able to understand the instructions, so I'd had to go over the road to her friend in order to fathom them. When I was fourteen, mother wanted me to do a needlework sampler – they were fashionable at the time. The shop-printed one I chose to do was printed so badly that I had to straighten it out and reposition the stitches before I could start sewing. Then while my sister was at university in the thirties she had no time to knit, so I did it for her. I remember making a beautiful jumper, with chromium-plated triangular buttons and faced revers. I even made her a black bathing-costume in a special bathing-costume wool, on number fourteen needles – a terrible job!

I grew up with the idea that brainwork was more important than craftwork; my dad and my sister were 'brainy'. But I liked doing creative

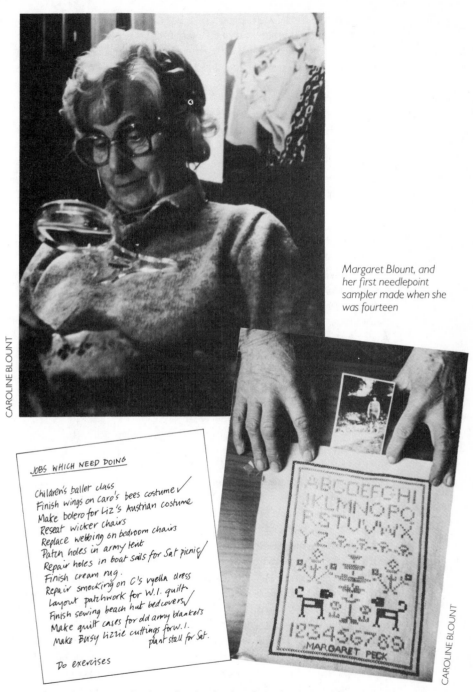

CAROLINE BLOUNT

Margaret Blount, and her first needlepoint sampler made when she was fourteen

CAROLINE BLOUNT

JOBS WHICH NEED DOING

Children's ballet class
Finish wings on Caro's bees costume ✓
Make bolero for Liz's Austrian costume
Reseat wicker chairs
Replace webbing on bedroom chairs
Patch holes in army tent
Repair holes in boat sails for Sat picnic ✓
Finish cream rug.
Repair smocking on C's vyella dress
Layout patchwork for W.I. quilt ✓
Finish sewing beach hut bedcovers ✓
Make quilt cases for old army blankets
Make Busy Lizzie cuttings for W.I.
                    plant stall for Sat.

Do exercises

My mother wrote endless lists of work to be done. It was important to 'reassure ourselves we're doing enough and achieving goals. But there's always something fresh – we never finish' things, and my family were proud of what I achieved. I'd have loved to have a Meccano set when I was a little girl; friends' brothers had them and I thought them fascinating. My father's elder sister did wood-carving, and I always wanted to do that too. I did needlework and cookery for the School Certificate. I wasn't as good as my sister at cookery, but I managed to retrieve my name a bit in the needlework.

C.: Was money an important factor?

M.: In our house there was never any spare money, so we didn't have new, 'bought' clothes. My auntie, working in America, brought back dress lengths, so home-sewn clothes were the nearest we got to 'new' ones. Mother spent a lot of time sewing and allocated all day Thursday to it. She made all our knickers, which were very fancy then, as well as petticoats and dresses. She even made us velvet dresses with second-hand sable trimmings. She often worked late into the night and I grew up thinking it normal. I now realise that it must have been very important to her that we looked respectable.

The other way we made clothes was by cutting down and re-sewing cast-offs from aunts and cousins. I was so used to this that there was a family joke about how, when little, I'd said on being given something new by mother, 'What was it before?' While I was a typist at Harriet Hubbard Ayer's cosmetic company, I made a dark-green wool suit with material bought from the Caledonian Market. But I couldn't afford a lining, so I took an old one out of my aunt's Harvey Nichols suit, leaving the label on; the girls at work thought I'd bought the whole suit there! The Caledonian Market also sold parachute silk and that was very useful for making French knickers, blouses and babies' underwear.

During the Second World War I did a lot of sewing and knitting for my sister and her son who were living with us, and a great deal of mending and making-do. Among the many tips the authorities gave out when there was a shortage of materials was the idea of re-making a deck-chair out of strips of webbing sewn together. I had a go at it and it lasted till 1969. Then I spent hours and hours darning my father's best grey suit which had got moth in it, especially in the worn and greasy parts. I spent hours imitating the herring-bone weave, but I shouldn't be surprised if he never wore it again. I suspect I only did it because my mother made me feel I ought to. My mother was very clever like that, foisting the nasty jobs on to me. It didn't occur to me that she might have done them herself, because she was convinced that she couldn't. My father used to say that I had 'an infinite capacity for taking pains': maybe he was right, but it wears a bit thin at times. The taking of pains to finish a job is somehow tied up with the morality of tidiness. I was taught not to tolerate things unfinished or unrepaired; I saw the leaving of things as a flaw in my make-up.

My mother was in the Women's Institute during the war, and she persuaded me to make a fisherman's oiled sweater, to send to the troops from the W.I.

C.: What do you enjoy now, about working as part of the W.I. Handicraft Committee?

M.: I really enjoy the bazaar work, and would do it ad infinitum if time was of no consequence. We've had some very friendly afternoons at some of our members' houses, chatting as we worked, all of us working on different pieces, or working together on something, like the patchwork quilt.

Most of the things we've made for bazaars over the years have been made from 'free' materials. I get a lot of satisfaction from making things that use spare materials; it's a matter of conservation. Sometimes I think that we take it a bit far, though; we spend too long thinking about how *not* to waste anything, and often what we're worrying about isn't worth using anyway. The things that sell best are those people would buy even if they weren't at a charity bazaar; things like cushion covers, needlework baskets, herb pillows, tea-cosies and soft toys. We do a lot of knitting, from unravelled and unwanted garments given to us by other W.I. members. Lately we've been making blanket squares for babies in hospital in Zambia.

We put a lot of time and skill into what we produce, and the results would be more special if we had really good materials to start with. Our work is limited by the narrow range of second-hand, offcut and sample materials we have. At the moment we are giving all the money we make to charity so each time we start the next batch of work for a bazaar, we don't have any resources to go and buy materials we'd really like. We meet a lot of resistance to our prices as it is – people expect bazaars to sell cheaper than elsewhere, so I don't think we can put up our prices.

I also cook flans and flapjacks for our W.I. food stall in the local market, and the nice thing about that is that I do get a contribution towards the food, even if it just goes towards the cost of using the oven. Much better, in my opinion, would be a system whereby women bartered the items, receiving in return other women's work; that's what I'd like.

MRS G. SWAIN

My grandmother, my mother and her doll, all three dressed in my grandmother's handiwork, 1917

Sue Scott

COUNTLESS HOURS
Grandmother's crochet

Here Sue Scott recounts her grandmother's skills in
crochet – small works of craft that are Sue's inheritance.
These are tiny mistresspieces, 'standing in' for so
many other consumed and used-up domestic
crafts. In these, the formal qualities have remained
to pass on the culture.

As I sit and knit I hear the faint echo of another pair of
needles clicking away in the back of my mind. As I link chain to chain in
my crochet I see my grandmother sitting in her armchair by the fire,
screwing up her eyes to catch the last of the daylight because 'the electric'
was never bright enough for her to work by. As I cut out patterns I hear
her scissors pulling across the table in the dining-room where she worked.
By these memories and by my craftwork I am inextricably bound to my
grandmother.

Born in 1888, the second of nine children, she spent her early years in
India and Sri Lanka, moving from place to place as her father's job as
station-master dictated. Whilst in India she was taught to crochet by one
of the local women in the traditional way, holding the hook at an angle, a
style which has been passed down to me by my mother. In 1896 she
returned to England with her family and settled in Norwich. At the age
of fourteen she had to choose a career for herself and decided to become
a tailoress. To this end she went as apprentice to a local tailor and, after
completing her training, remained there until she married. Following the
custom dictated by the marriage ban, she then left work to become a
full-time wife and mother.

At the outbreak of the First World War her husband was called up,
leaving her to manage as best she could with a young baby to care for.
Although she had the usual wife's allowance from her husband's army pay,
she soon found that it was not enough to live on in any degree of comfort.
The options open to her were few. She could work in the munitions
factory as did her sister Beatrice, but this would mean leaving her baby
for long periods of time. Alternatively, she could 'take in' soldiers, these
men being the overflow from the local army barracks who needed a roof
over their heads and good food on the table. Finding no attraction in

either of these choices, she decided to put her previous training to good use by starting her own business working from home as a tailoress. In this way she would remain at home with her child and, to some extent, be in control of the number of hours she worked and when she worked them.

The income from this work provided her with a few creature comforts plus the materials which she needed to practise her other craft, crochet. When work was scarce she economised by using sewing thread instead of crochet cotton, and soon came to prefer this for delicate work. This practice was to take its toll in later years when her eyes began to fail due to the strain of so much 'close work'. My mother has several cheval sets made at this time which must have taken her countless hours of painstaking work to complete. A table cloth edged with flamboyant peacocks worked in white crochet cotton, exquisite crocheted gloves which she made for herself and her young daughter to wear with their summer dresses – all this was accomplished in her spare minutes between housework, cooking, washing and tailoring.

As her daughter grew she began to teach her to crochet, knit and sew: part of a young girl's basic education in preparation for her future married life. She started her daughter's training with simple pulled-thread work on sheets and pillowcases, finishing the more difficult parts herself, so that many pieces were joint efforts between mother and daughter.

Her tiny house at the end of the terrace was filled to overflowing with her work. When I stayed with her during the school holidays I slept

Examples of my grandmother's fine crocheted tablecloths worked in white cotton

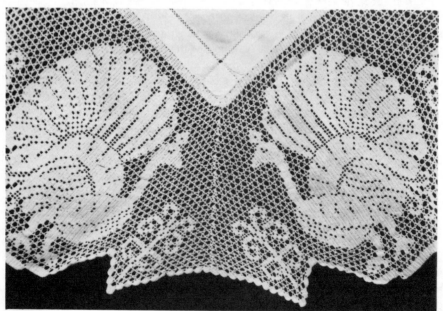

DAVID ROBERTS

between starched white cotton sheets with deep picot edging. The curtains hanging at the window had been made on her treadle sewing machine which stood against the wall opposite my bed. Every room in that house bore her signature in the form of some piece of crochet work or sewing. The result was a warmth and feeling of security which pervaded the entire house and travelled with you when you left it.

She passed her skills of crochet, tailoring, sewing and knitting down to her daughter, who in turn taught my two sisters and myself. For a while during my teens I chose to ignore the family craft traditions in favour of mass-produced goods. It was considered old-fashioned to knit, and dowdy to wear home-made clothes. It was not until after my grandmother's death that I came to realise, too late, just what I had missed. When I wanted to produce a particular effect in a piece of work, I knew that she would have understood what I wanted and known the answer, but I had lost the opportunity to ask her. Slowly, as I began to pick up the threads of my knowledge, I began to realise the value of the craft traditions practised by the women of my family. Now that I have returned to craftwork after a long period of inactivity, I find that it is not only a pleasure but also a comfort when times are bad. In an ever-changing world there is something permanent and unfaltering in a piece of craftwork which waits for you to return to it at the end of a busy day. In the 1980s my life is comparatively free from the domestic drudgery which my grandmother had to work through in order to emerge at the end of the day with time

DAVID ROBERTS

to spare for her craftwork. I have more choice in what I do because I have more money to spare and more free time in which to work.

However, so much of women's lives is still filled with repetitive service work, meals prepared and eaten, clothes washed, ironed and soiled again, rooms tidied and then cluttered. These works of craft may be subject to wear and tear in daily use but they are some of the few lasting reminders of women's skills. Visiting an antiques fair recently I saw great piles of crochet mats selling for between £1.00 and £2.50. The prices seemed ridiculously low for this labour-intensive work: £1.50 for a mat which must have taken five hours to make costs out at 30p per hour for skilled work. We should treasure these tiny works of craft created by our mothers and grandmothers in time salvaged from a life of hard work, time used to create something of beauty for their own pleasure. How much more precious are these pieces of work than 'priceless masterpieces' hanging in galleries and laden with honours?

Agnes and Kate Walker

STARTING WITH RAG RUGS
The aesthetics of survival

Craftwork performed by women within a domestic setting has been done for love and for creative need, and also for the domestic economy: it is an aesthetic of survival. Apart from the occasional sale to the 'rag-and-bone' man, mentioned here by Agnes Walker, women have creatively re-cycled everything in the home by a process of demotion – jacket to rug to doormat, and blouse to polisher to floor-cloth. Here, Kate Walker and her mother Agnes speak of their craftwork.

Kate: My mother talked to me a lot during my childhood about the handiwork of both my grandmothers. Emily Walker was a 'non-working' mother of four who learned all kinds of skills thorugh her life in service at the 'big house' of the local squire. Agnes McHale was an Irish immigrant and deserted mother of five who put every ounce of her skills to use as a paid worker. She was a cook and a highly skilled maker of crocheted garments. As an artist I find that all my female relatives have influenced my attitudes. I, like my mother, maintain some scepticism about the rediscovery of craftwork because for working-class women, any nostalgia about it is bogus. Exploited, unpaid work was the very thing that my grandmothers left North Yorkshire and County Mayo to escape. My mother and I are all too aware that although we respect the skills passed on to us, they stink of poverty. It is impossible to pretend that those objects were 'good works' or 'art'. In those days your work was used, trodden on, or worn right out, like you yourself.

I spoke to my mother, and my questioning started with rag rugs.

Agnes: First you get your hessian – we used washed potato sacks which, if we were lucky, we got free from the local shop, or sometimes your dad got them from his work lorry-driving. Then you take your rag strips – we mainly used cast-off outer clothes. There weren't jumble sales in our day, where we lived; occasionally we would sell a few things to the rag-and-bone man for some coppers, but mostly we used everything up ourselves; everybody did, so there wasn't anything to go in a jumble sale. The outer garments went into the rugs, the underwear was used as cleaning rags, and the woollens were unpicked and knitted up again. Some people who made rugs used to swap stuff, for the sake of the colours to make up a pattern; your grandmother used to do that with great glee.

You use a rag hook to poke the strips into the hessian backing; you can imagine it as darning the hessian, but leaving loops which form the pile of the rug. There were two or three working methods: you could cut short strips, which I always did because it was quicker. You just prod one strip at a time, leaving the two ends to form the pile; it made a loose, floppy rug. But your grandmother always used a long strip; she prodded it in about an inch and a half on each side of the hessian, making a completely reversible rug that was very heavy. They were very difficult to lift and shake; we used to clean them by banging them against the wall, but it took more than one person to bang grandma's rugs.

Your grandmother always had a rug on the go during the winter, and she'd put a new one down on the hearth every spring, and move the older ones upstairs. When they got too worn, she'd cut off the good bits to use as mats. She made quite complicated patterns by drawing round plates and saucers and things. Your Auntie Ivy took some of the rugs after she died, but she didn't keep them long; everyone was saying at the funeral, 'Fancy taking those old things!' In the end she burnt them because

'Girly Art', a banner by Kate Walker

J. T. McSHANE

RHONDA WILSON

Rag rugs in traditional style

people thought that, being home-made, they were common. But in your grandmother's day, there wasn't anything you could buy; you were poor, you made your own pillow-slips and everything. They put them out from the age of twelve; she was in service from then, till she married. Imagine, from that to your own home, your own things. She was very house-proud, though she got everything second-hand.

My rugs were never masterpieces like your grandma's. I used mainly navy blue, with bits of red here and there. You used to save the bright bits for the corners, and you used to look at other people's rugs, and your own old ones, for ideas. But I never had much time for rug-making, just the evenings sometimes, when I wasn't knitting or decorating, or just washing. Washing was hellish! There was no hot water in the house; you had to heat it all up in the copper, what we called the set-pot. First you had to light a fire under it, then when the water was hot, you had to ladle it out by hand, into the peggy tub. There was no soap powder in those days, only this green soap that you shredded. So when I was working, I didn't have much time for the rugs, but I always knitted a lot.

Kate: Behind the questions to my mother was the tangle in my head of a childhood rooted in a different visual culture from the notions of 'art' in the world in which I now mostly live. In my own work I have used knitting, embroidery and quilting in an ironic and semi-detached way, to try and say something about the tangle – this inter-relation of women's work with art, with class, with leisure.

Pen Dalton

HOUSEWIVES, LEISURE CRAFTS AND IDEOLOGY
De-skilling in consumer craft

The media images of craftwork are of occupations
for 'spare' time, tasks which express in the process
and confirm in the product a suitable view of
femininity. Here Pen Dalton writes about craft
companies who penetrate both the private space of
home and the institutional world of school, to
produce consumer craftwork. The craft is taken
from its functional and formal roots, simplified and
de-skilled, then sold back as a package of tuition,
patterns, materials, magazines and books. This then
has the doubly oppressive result of keeping people
quietly occupied at home, happily replicating the
'feminine' image of unpaid dainty work.

The image of mum knitting by the fireside while dad
reads the newspaper and the kids play quietly together continues to hold
its place as a picture of an ideal of family life. As far as the housewife is
concerned, this ideal has a basis in reality since women do, in fact, spend
a great deal of their leisure hours in crafts, of which knitting is the most
popular. It is an image that is reinforced by the mass media where there
is an implicit assumption that leisure crafts are practised by housewives,
heterosexual females living in a nuclear family unit. 'Knit his 'n hers
sweaters', 'A pretty layette for baby' and 'Bean bags for the boys' are
typical titles of craft projects to be found in women's magazines which
serve to reproduce and support the 'norm' of the nuclear family unit and
the place and function of woman within it.

These craft projects also represent the advancement of a growing
leisure industry. Along with other home-based activities such as gardening
and DIY, crafts are on the increase, and specialist magazines and pro-
motions in the mass media serve to create and stimulate interest as well
as demands for textiles, patterns, books, kits, materials and equipment.
The positive result of this has been the stimulation of interest and awareness

in crafts and the re-activation of craft skills and techniques, but it can also be argued that the encouraging of dependence on projects from women's magazines, patterns and pre-designed kits, however well designed and demanding of the patience and skill of the housewife, has had a standardising and largely detrimental effect on craft practice. Women look to magazines, books and kits for ideas and aesthetic stimulus; the notion that crafts could represent their own ideas, values, experiences and fantasies has no place in leisure craft ideologies.

Leisure crafts, as represented in women's magazines, are qualitatively different from professional or vocational crafts. A professional craftworker, it is assumed, is usually trained at an art college or has served some kind of apprenticeship with the award of a legitimate status or degree at the end of it. Professional craftworkers can learn their skills in the world of work, sale and exchange, in the context of competition, display and exhibition. They may, like the housewife, work alone, but are able to communicate through professional publications and societies, exhibition outlets, employment and critical exchanges; they keep abreast of contemporary markets, and technical and aesthetic issues.

The housewife's main social and economic contacts are with her immediate family, friends and neighbours and the world of consumption and advertising. It is likely that her main aesthetic stimulus comes from her schooling, television and women's magazines. It is difficult for a woman with small children to attend meetings, to travel, to wander around exhibitions or to browse in libraries. Women's magazines are delivered through the door, they are already *concerned* with women's problems in the home and family and they are ready at hand.

The discourse of leisure crafts represented in these magazines and on afternoon television has its own ideological assumptions about the nature of crafts, of leisure and 'the housewife'. It is through and in these representations, amongst others, that women construct their identities as feminine, as mothers, as craftworkers and as housewives. Implicit in these assumptions are notions of women as carers, as responsible for the harmony, beauty and comfort of the home. Their craft practice is not professional, but is represented as a means of giving and gaining love, as offerings for the family, presents for others or as gifts for charity bazaars. In practising these crafts women renew and confirm themselves in the identity of 'housewife'.

Men, women without children or husbands, lesbians, ethnic minorities are excluded from these representations as are the less popular aspects of family life. The usual frustrations and irritations, the stress, death, loss, separation, poverty, lack of privacy, divided interests and social tensions which are part of so much family life are not considered suitable subjects for expression in craftwork. In popular discourse, leisure crafts are bound up with the superficial, the solely decorative, and transient values. Women assume that their own ideas, feelings and experiences have no valid relation to the things they make, that their work cannot be considered 'art'. Even when women have shown amazing skill, creativity and artistry in knitting or sewing, it has been difficult for them to evaluate their own work as 'skill' or 'art'; so long have textile crafts been women's work that they have been regarded as an extension of femininity itself or, at best, a different kind of housework.

These ideological associations are re-activated and constantly repro-duced in women's magazines, but in early childhood girls are familiar with the association of leisure crafts with housewives. In her childhood the little girl has probably been given a sewing kit whilst her brother has a tool set. In schooling the conditioning process continues to train the young woman into habits and skills that make the association between women and textiles a natural one. In public examinations at school, in spite of attempts to include boys in the textile crafts, girls continue to dominate; the subject continues, less explicitly, to be taught as a girls' craft. In the new 'Craft, Design and Technology' examination, materials such as metal, wood, plastic, fabric, food and clay are accorded equal value and status in the examination system – 'a culinary recipe is a design, so is a musical or chronological score. These, together with flow charts, computer programs and knitting patterns are a special kind of design called algorithms'.[1] In effect, the inequality is just hidden: although awarded equal status in school examinations, in the real world of jobs, status and money, computer experts have a different value and status than do knitting experts. Through the curriculum girls learn their potential place as consumers. Fashion and textile manufacturers such as those who produce 'Style' and 'Simplicity' patterns have realised the advantages of establishing habits and brand loyalties in young girls, and have for many years quietly and effectively promoted and supported textile and consumer craft education. They have supplied home economics departments of schools with project proposals, wall charts, visual aids and cheap patterns which teachers, especially since educational cuts, have eagerly accepted. Girls are carefully and systematically guided through a pre-designed, pre-cut paper pattern for a garment or soft toy. After five years, although they may have mastered considerable sewing skills, they are unable to design and construct a simple garment of their own choice, but are dependent on patterns produced by fashion industries. From school they move on to familiar patterns produced by the same manufacturers, in women's magazines. In art and design teaching, where children supposedly exercise creative and imaginative faculties, there is lip service given to a notion of 'self-expression'. In practice it is the teacher, with the aid of textbooks, project notes and theories from art education research, who determines what is or is not a suitable subject to learn. It is the child's task to think of 'creative' ways of solving the teacher's problems; in contemporary art education theory, this is known as 'the Design Process'. Children's own problems are not considered as suitable for expression in the art/craft classroom. Personal relationships, family problems, school work, ill health, sex and all the other things with which one imagines children to be preoccupied do not appear as subjects for art and craftwork. Nor do the other things which determine the quality of children's lives: the law, divorce, violence, the concept of childhood itself are not 'expressed' in these lessons. Children learn art and crafts as something outside their own preoccupations, interests and values; they thus distrust their own perceptions and can debase their understandings. With a tendency to rely on others for patterns and designs and with a deep mistrust of her own ideas, it is not surprising that the young woman looks to the 'expert' in women's magazines for help and advice in craftwork. In effect, the voice of the housewife, her experience, emotions and values are suppressed. The work of the housewife does not appear on television culture shows, it receives no critical attention or academic interest and there are few well funded exhibitions or prominent public displays of the housewife's craft.

Since the rise of the current feminist movement there have been the beginnings of a re-evaluation of the work of women in the home. There are now women trained as artists who have high professional expectations and confidence in their own abilities but, in common with other housewives, they may find themselves cut off by domestic ties from dominant cultural practices. These women have rejected the art values and 'professionalism' learned at art institutions, and have led a movement among women to find out a new line of art/craft practice which does not separate them from daily life, its affections and problems, its values and vital

SU RICHARDSON

Su Richardson's 'Aloe Variegata Mucho Exotica!' and seeds. Crocheted cotton, wool and lurex potplant from the Postal Event

From the Postal Event

MICHAEL ANN MULLEN

concerns. The results have been alternative crafts which have attempted to communicate the material and political condition of the housewife based on personal experience. In 1976 the *Postal Event: Portrait of the Artist as Housewife* was shown in Manchester (described by Su Richardson on p. 39). In this event women, trained and untrained, communicated with each other in the media of domestic crafts, representing their lives and work as housebound mothers and wives. The exhibition toured widely and was shown as 'art' at the Institute of Contemporary Arts in London. Since then, there have been other domestic craft-based exhibitions: *Mother's Pride, Mother's Ruin* was first shown in 1977; *Fenix* in 1980; *The Breadline Women's Craft Exhibition* in 1979 and 1980; *Women Textile Artists: their Lives and their Work* in 1983. *The Dinner Party* by Judy Chicago and others has been exhibited in the UK; it has brought a view of homeworkers and embroiderers, projecting domestic skills into a wider social context.

I would not want to promote the idea that the 'correct' craft practice for women is to aim to exhibit in galleries or to be accepted into the existing standards and values of the art world: the fact that women's craftwork is private and personal is vital, and to a great extent determines the media, the scale, the content and the work's formal properties. The fact that much of it is done for pleasure, for love and *not* for competition, exhibition or sale, is part of its strength and value. But I also believe it is important that such work should be seen by a wide audience. The reasons for this are, first, because it provides evidence of women's culture and history, evidence which can mean stimulus and encouragement for craft-workers. Secondly, craftwork's existence, and the lives of women who make it, provide a challenge to the established notions of 'great art' and 'great artist'. (It has long been a popular belief that 'art' is produced by 'great' individuals in special circumstances.) Thirdly, it is important to show housewives' craftwork because it brings to the fore those values which have been missing from the cultural scene – caring, modesty, gentleness. These are not necessarily feminine characteristics, but they have, through cultural association, been most successfully represented by women. Finally, communicating through craft can give the woman tied to the home a voice outside to penetrate and influence the dominant sphere of cultural exchange. Only the housewife can give an authentic account of her life, work and material conditions. Unless we speak out, and in any form available to us, we can never hope to gain access to the means of owning and controlling the institutions of power that circumscribe and determine our lives as housewives. It is up to us as critics, artists, craftworkers and feminists to seek out and support such work, discuss and criticise it and construct a new category of leisure crafts that is the authentic voice of the housewife herself, and to have the confidence to assess, to reject or to use the consumer crafts in women's magazines to meet only our own identified needs and desires.

Su Richardson talks to Gaie Davidson

CROCHETED STRATEGIES

A new audience for women's work

Su Richardson has found a new audience for women's work – that of women. Some of this audience emerged through the Postal Event which she describes here. Su lives with her son and her partner in Birmingham; now a self-employed musician, she crochets and knits just for fun.

I first started making things as a child. I remember sitting in the back of the car fiddling around with press-studs and needles and little bits of thread, and making tiny dolls' clothes, and making houses for dolls, and generally constructing things. I went through school and art college, teacher training, then teaching myself, managing not to get involved much with craft, nor even art. It wasn't until after I had a child that I started to do any work, and that only came about because I was so frustrated with being at home all the time. Earlier, I had learnt from someone how to crochet, so I crocheted a few clothes for my son. I put a lot of effort into it, thought about the colours I was using, and designed different sorts of garments for him. Then I wanted to do something just for me; it was to do with trying to reclaim my own identity. So six months after his birth I made a huge wall-hanging, with him rolling all over the bits on the floor as I made it. Eventually we got it up on the wall, and I found its vast size very satisfying. A woman friend pointed out that its imagery was concerned with birth and creation, and with being female. I was surprised and unsure about the comment but nevertheless found it encouraging. Later, I began to think that maybe this fine art had got some use after all, and I bore it in mind.

I didn't make any more work for a time, but I did involve myself with other women in the Birmingham Women Artists' Group. We met to talk about our experiences, our energies and our activities; we found that much of our creativity was directed towards cooking the tea, or making clothes, and choosing things – more practical areas than those of fine art. Some of us went to a 'Women in Art History' conference in London; I think I went along just to be with the others. There I heard Kate Walker talking. She was frustrated by some long-winded discussion and she said

'Bear It In Mind' by Su Richardson, from the Postal Event/Fenix *exhibitions*

CAROLINE BLOUNT

suddenly, 'Look, aren't there any housewives here who want to make some art, and who are fed up with all this fine art business? Aren't there any of you making things at home that you'd like to show each other?' And I thought to myself 'Yes.' So we in Birmingham got together with Kate and others, and joined to make the Postal Event. We sent little art works through the post to each other. We didn't worry about finish, we just made them; we used whatever little time we had, whatever materials and skills were available. It was making art out of the bits and pieces in between the nappies and washing-up. It was a revelation. I found so much in myself that had been hidden and repressed, so much resentment at the way I'd been treated as a woman, and I discovered that other women's work was coming back to me in the same vein, using often the same imagery. We'd found a commonality; it gave us strength, this shared experience and expression of being female in a male-oriented society. We'd found our audience in each other. I think art is a way of recording experience and passing it on, but for a long time, in the visual arts, the communication has been for men.

Through the Postal Event experience I was led to involvement with the creative process; what I made was no longer just its formal qualities, colours or textures, but something of reason and purpose. It was often

'Broken Heart Rug' by Su Richardson

RHONDA WILSON

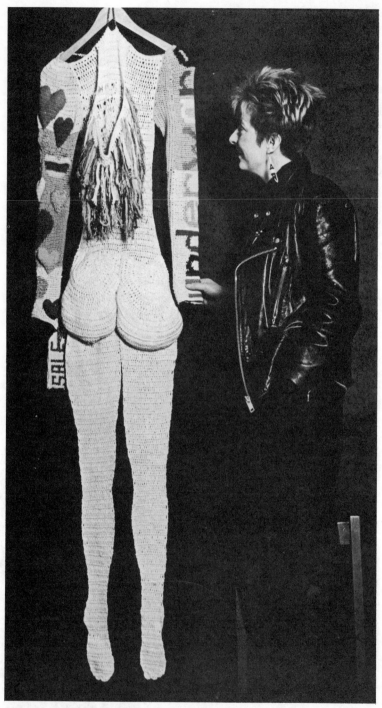

'Underwear – Skin Sale' by Su Richardson

RHONDA WILSON

cynically humorous, too. I've since used a lot of crochet: it's a medium I can control; I didn't learn it from a man, and men don't know enough about it to pass comment. It's a medium that's always been connected with women and with the female experience; as a womanly craft it's generally had a utility purpose too. So I make jackets about peace and cushions about super-wonderwoman. Another example of my work is my underwear piece: it's a crocheted skin with a padded bottom and a nice wig-hat. You can wear it – it's got arms, and feet that trail behind; one of the arms has padded hearts sewn all over, the other has 'underwear' written on it, and a label which says 'skin' on one side, and 'sale' on the other. It's to do with being a woman in a street, particularly at night; being looked at, followed, commented on, talked at, as an object. Then we become just a skin of a certain size and shape; with this piece I've tried to reveal a skin, and reverse the process.

Elaine Thomas

CRAFT OF CARNIVAL

Again, unlike the pre-packaged consumer craft, we
can see here the dynamism of a craft that, though
transplanted, is still securely rooted to a functional
role. Elaine Thomas has been making costumes for the
Chapeltown Carnival in Leeds for some time; she
has lived in Britain for many years, though she was
born in Jamaica. Here she talks about how she got
involved in costume-making, about the making the
of the costumes, and what both mean to her.

I was first invited to the Carnival just to watch – I went
along with a group of girls and was gripped by it. We all of us thoroughly
enjoyed it but I know that the impact on me was enormous. Somebody
once said that when you're black, and you hear a drum beat, you just can't
sit still – Carnival is like that for me, and there's all the colour of the
costumes as well. I know that I shall want to be involved in it for the rest
of my life. It's not obvious really, because I wasn't brought up with it.
Carnival originated in Africa, and we took it westward with us. But in the
West Indies, Trinidad is the biggest on Carnival; where Jamaica is famous
for reggae, Trinidad has Carnival. The giant of all Carnivals is in Brazil, and
that's what I dream of. I'm only the third generation out of Africa, but still,
at home in Jamaica, I had no idea of this tradition; it took Chapeltown to
show me.

In Carnival you have queens, and troupes to go with each, wearing
simplified versions of the queen costume. The queens themselves are
transformed into birds, flowers, suns and so on. We have some magnificent
costumes in Leeds, and it seems to me that over the years they've got better
and better. We have competitions just between the Leeds costumes, and
when it comes to Carnival, there might be four or five queens from
different parts of town. Then there might be one queen each from
Huddersfield, Bradford and Birmingham, and perhaps one from Preston.
The queen costumes are judged on the August bank holiday weekend at
a big dance with the Lord Mayor of Leeds and visitors from all over. On
the Monday there's a parade from the park down into town, and back up
Chapeltown Road, everyone dancing all the way; and then there's another
dance in the evening, and that's where you can see a total display of all

TELEGRAPH & ARGUS

Vibrant costume at the Leeds carnival

the costumes.

Well, the second time I went along with a group of girls we all got dressed up, just in average costumes, a troupe without a queen. Then I was asked if I would like to make a queen costume next time. I've been involved in dressmaking – I make clothes and soft toys – but this was altogether more. I started from a name: I'd always been fascinated by birds and I decided to call my costume 'Bird of Paradise'. Then I had to think of how to go about building a costume that a woman could possibly dance in. I wanted it the way I saw it in my imagination, which wasn't with a beak and that sort of thing, but I can't draw – I can tell you what I think, but I can't put it down on paper. I go along thinking, that's too long, or that's not long enough – it's so frustrating. It's frustrating as well for a joiner or whoever, who's trying to help me, because I get lost when it comes to measurement, balance, and things like that. My husband's a joiner and I know he finds it impossible to work without exact measurements. I've been told I could go along to an art college and perhaps they'd help me, but I haven't done that yet. We do need a workshop where someone could show us the technical side of what we want, because we're all just people like me, average housewives or people who work, just people who do it for the love of it.

The costumes are getting bigger and more elaborate, and often have to be built in three or four sections – that's where the joiner or welder comes in, to put the costumes together. And, too, they have to be put away and stored while you're making them. You might start building in a garage, but everything else has to come out of it, and it might contain only half the costume anyway. I made one costume in a school, but the rest I've tried my best to make at home. When I do it at home, the girls can work till 11 or 12 at night; last time there were twelve or thirteen working on it. To get the girls to work on it, I put a notice up in the youth clubs, or ask the youth leader to put the word about. When I have the list of names, I tell their parents about it all and get permission for them to work on it. Generally I use wire and fabric and tinsel; some people use papier-mâché and fur – one winning costume was made of tights material. Even though the costumes fill the street – when they come up it, nothing else goes by – they have to be light enough for the queens to walk a long way. And, at the same time, they mustn't be too big for the stage at the judging.

After Carnival the winning costume will be kept for publicity and display; the others are usually abandoned. I used to hang on to mine so that the children could see them – I think it's important to pass these things on to another generation, so the skills, and the roots, don't get lost. After I first saw Carnival in Leeds I went along to the library to see if there were any books on it. I couldn't find a thing. There were books on costume, but they were all British, which is not the same thing at all. There was not one book, magazine or photograph – nothing. More recently, someone on the Carnival Committee has acquired film of the big one that's held in Rio every year. What we really need are videos of the film in order to take our time studying the costumes and events. We need videos for our children as well, to teach them about Carnival. We'd like to have a workshop here in Leeds, so that we can pass our skills and knowledge on to our children. People have a love of the West Indies; we can't keep them here in Britain – one of our very talented costume makers, Idris Brown, has just gone home. Maybe the rest of us will go back too, and then the younger generation of blacks will die into the English system, another part of their roots completely forgotten.

It's good to think of Carnival as a day out and a chance to let your hair down, but for us it's more than that because it celebrates our roots and provides us with a way of developing our culture.

Shirley Cameron

KNITTING
PERFORMANCES

Shirley Cameron has moved from the palaces of
fine art culture to parks, marketplaces and agricultural
fairs. She has transformed her sculptor's media,
such as metal and wood, to women's craft materials,
such as wool and icing-sugar. With these she has
made performances. Shirley lives in Sheffield with
her twin daughters and has often overcome the
difficulties of combining outside work with child-care
by incorporating her daughters into her
performances. Here she writes about knitting.

I have worked on and off as a performance artist for
the last fourteen years. In the course of working this way, I have presented
in public several 'performances' in which I have used knitting.

Originally, in the sixties, I worked as a sculptor with hard materials –
metal, plastic and wood – and I exhibited this work in galleries where I
found I received very little response or feedback about my work and
ideas. I had a full-time (non-art) job, and I needed a way of making art
that took up less time (and money), which could be presented to people
who didn't visit galleries (which most people don't), and which would
produce a direct response from the people seeing it. I wanted to go on
making interesting things for people to look at, but I wanted to be around
to see what they thought, to be involved there and then with my work,
and to answer questions if necessary. My 'fine art' ideas, developed in the
course of a lengthy education, I wanted to make accessible to others. The
way of working I adopted only later came to be called 'performance art',
so it could be said that my ambitions – as I have described them above –
helped to produce a new way of working.

This sounds grand, but a lot of my work has been modest enough, as
with the first time I used knitting-in-public as an element in my work.
Appropriately here, it took place in an upper room of a craft shop, run
by a friend in Swansea where I lived then, in 1970. No doubt the craft
shop itself gave me the idea of using knitting because of its crafted objects,
its attractiveness, its coloured wools – that, together with my desire for
what I was doing to 'fit in' and seem normal, and therefore accessible.

I agreed to be in the shop for a whole week from 10 am to 5 pm, which was a long time. A connection is that stitches seem to measure time: a stitch a second, so many a minute, and in a whole day? Well, a lot of knitting. Before the start of the week of public presentation I sub-divided the room with translucent coloured plastic panels, triangular in shape. The first area was red where I did my red and maroon and pink and crimson knitting. Then there was a blue, and then a green and a yellow area where likewise I knitted in these colour ranges. On the floor were bottles of drink painted with toning colours, and visitors would be offered a drink and would talk with me and sometimes add to the knitting. If they returned later in the week, as quite a few did, they would find less drink and much more knitting all around. The performance both symbolised and lived through the domestic activity of knitting as a social experience.

More specifically about 'time' was a performance I did with two friends in Holland. The subject was again the measurement of time; and I used yellow and red colours for the wool, clothes, trolley, candle, bats – all the paraphernalia we used in the performance. We set up along a path in a public park, where a hundred-metre length of yellow wool was to be knitted by the seated woman (me), while at the other end of the hundred metres a small trolley with a candle in the centre was attached to the wool. The metres were marked along the wool, as were rings around the candle, so time and distance were measured. People gathered round to watch the trolley slowly moving towards me, and the slowly growing knitting. After half an hour, the trolley finally reached the knitter. To make a link between 'end' and 'end', also to stress the importance of the process of knitting as opposed to the resulting product and definitively to signal the end of the presentation, I then burned the knitting with the candle. It flared up in an instant.

'Ropes', a knitting performance in Antwerp, 1973

Knitting can be a way of actually linking different threads together, and as such can also create a symbol of that linking. In 'Spiderwoman' I was up above the foyer of the building where the 1979 Leicester Women's Festival was being held, sitting on a ladder balanced from ledge to ledge across the foyer. Below, on the walls of the area, was a small exhibition; the four works in it were made of white ribbon stretched across and across frames. The framed ribbon panels each contained biographical information on four women, written on the ribbon itself; one of them was about my own life. Each had a length of that ribbon extending up to where I sat, just above the heads of the people coming into the building, walking from room to room, buying things. I was dressed as Spiderwoman in black with extra legs, and I was knitting the threads of the four lives together, but I talked as myself, explaining what I was doing. After my day on the ladder, the festival went on and my contribution stayed as an exhibit with the panels half-knitted away, and the ribbons extending above to where the knitting was hung. I know that what Spiderwoman had done that first day, and the image of it, was carried on by the explanations of the women who had seen it to those, later in the festival, who had not.

Three years ago, I was invited to be one of the artists presenting their work to the public in a park in Kassel, Germany. The strongest work I performed there was, I believe, 'Tree Knitting'. I was dressed in a dark suit, but with yellow face and hair, red hands holding red knitting needles and wool, and blue painted feet. I had climbed a beautiful tall tree, leaving blue footprints up its trunk. My friend tied the long lengths of yellow wool, which was my hair, on to branches near to and far from where I sat, until I was completely joined to the tree. And then for hours I sat in my tree knitting the red wool, so that the red knitting grew longer and longer, and nearer and nearer to the ground. People looked up and stood around, asking each other what folk-tale I was representing, how long I had been there, guessing what would happen when my knitting reached the ground, and so on. They would walk round the park, and when they returned I was still there. When at last it did reach the ground, I brought out a knife, cut myself free, and climbed down to the piece of ground that my knitting had reached. There I talked with some of my audience.

I believe that these four 'performances', although all of course different, do use a combination of the familiar, that-which-can-be-identified-with (i.e. the knitting women), and the unfamiliar, the strange and unexpected. This is why the performances are interesting, but not intimidating. They all use the attractive qualities of coloured wools or ribbon, combined with special costumes, and they make patterns and meanings with the people, objects and activities used. They take place in publicly accessible spaces where people are free to stay and watch or wander around or away. They make public one more area of women's private unseen activity and, though they are small-scale events, my knitting performances do celebrate this activity.

Alison, Bridget, Daphne, Eileen and Michele, recorded by Su Richardson

PEACE BANNER CONVERSATIONS
Discussions from a sewing bee

We are women who formed together out of an initial joining with others of the Women and Multi-Media Group in Birmingham. That group has been a meeting-point for women in all arts media to exchange information, form networks, make links; and it has cut across differences in age, experience, circumstance, skill, as well as medium. Our sewing bee was one of many groupings which linked through those meetings. These conversations took place as we sat around Daphne's kitchen table, and in her sunny garden. It was time taken for ourselves, to listen, laugh, share, sew, knit and patch together our feelings and thoughts in a 'banner for peace'.

Su: Making banners for peace, together, feels to me like a truly feminine way forward. We're using a female art form, we're publicly demonstrating our women's skills, our communal method of working is an ancient one, and we're conveying our new message of peace.

Daphne: Like sewing bees. Years ago, economic necessity made sewing a legitimate way for women to spend time together. I think we're rediscovering the value of that practice.

Su: I was thinking about how we seem able to discuss important issues in depth, while making our squares, swapping skills and ideas and that, all sitting round a kitchen table. Here we can learn from each other without competing, and although we're all broadly working to the same theme, we're materialising very different images. Maybe our images will speak specially to women.

Daphne: Most of us are very divorced from visual languages; they seem so separated from everyday experience. Myself, I've always needed to practise creative skills. When times are really bad, I sew or garden; the clear product of clothes or vegetables is helpful.

Bridget: I've always been good at crafts, but my whole focus has been

Eileen with a Labour Party banner

on painting and drawing. I've sat and knitted jumpers and felt I was wasting time, away from things more intellectual. I've internalised male value judgements. I think that we women start out from a different place from men, and then we try to reach their standards, strive to get to where they started from.

Su: Maybe you could make a long knitted statement about it.

Bridget: Well, I certainly came unstuck when I tried a photographic statement. I was in a consciousness-raising group, within which I did a photographic project on vaginas. We were all interested in the way the images didn't look pornographic. They were our bodies as they are. But when I exhibited the photographs, the feedback from men was devastating; most of them seemed to feel actually sick.

Su: I think there's a problem in using photography as a medium for feminism when it involves images of women, because it's been used so much to portray women's bodies in objectified bits.

Daphne: Yes, but exhibiting is important, and selling too, and all we've got is the male world to do it in. Do you know, as a craftswoman, I don't even earn enough to rent a workshop? All my earnings do for me is enable me to carry on buying the materials.

Eileen: When I was making trade union banners, they helped subsidise the other banners I did for a song.

Daphne: And I don't expect you were working to union rates!

Eileen: Oh no! I don't think union rates exist for banner-makers.

Daphne: But we've all got to earn something or we can't go on doing it.

SU RICHARDSON

The Women for Peace banner made by the Women and Multi-Media Group in Birmingham

Michele: Very few women are financially independent. We need a few more wealthy women around, patronesses.

Eileen: But I feel inadequate about my work anyhow, so it's difficult to think of charging much for it. I mean, most of the women in this group have had some sort of training; as a result you all feel, and I do too, that you can command a price. I've just done a bit here and there, codged up this and that in a higgledy-piggledy way.

Daphne: But what that means is that you've had to think things out for yourself – you're used to finding your own creative solutions, away from established tram-lines.

Michele: That's what women have always done, isn't it?

Eileen: Yes, I suppose we've had to improvise, having little to dispose of, and most of what we've made has been for use. My mother was a good needlewoman, but she limited herself to those awful gymslips and to cookery aprons.

Michele: Perhaps we're rebelling against that now, in doing things for our pleasure. On the other hand, the origins of art are religious icons for religious functions. We don't have that any more.

Alison: But my craft is essential to myself. I don't need to make blankets for their warmth, nor do I need to sell them for the money. But for the health of my spirit, I need to decorate my blankets.

Michele: But it gives art a different function when it's decorated afterwards, it gives it extra significance of religious power. I think that most art made now isn't rooted in that sort of experience, it's art just for art's sake and difficult for us to see it having any other value.

Alison: Yes, for the audience art's been moved from the personal, to become an object 'out there'.

Eileen: I think we make things to show that we've existed, so that there will be something left of us when we're gone. Even a crocheted blanket can be passed on.

Alison: On the other hand, we as women have always taken care of men's physical wellbeing, so that they can get on with the creative business; they have the things to pass on and they call it 'culture'.

Eileen: But there are lots of men involved in very menial work, down sewers, in factories, working on the bins. They need to be freed from that sort of work too, in order to participate in 'culture', or even in the creative, nurturing work of women.

Alison: The point is that it's going to be a long time before either men or women will be free in ways that we want, and in the meantime our attitudes must change, or those working conditions won't either.

Michele: That's why I think women's struggles and the making of statements are important. That's why I'm involved with this banner, why I put my energy here. For me, we women working together, our images about growth and expansion, our political statements – these things need to be made visible. That's what our banner will do.

The 'Women for Peace' banner was completed and taken to Greenham Common. It has since been used at other women's events and exhibited with other banners. We felt our group had fulfilled its purpose and, though we remain in contact, we have all now moved on to other activities and areas of work.

PART TWO

ARTY
CRAFT
AND
CRAFTY
ART

THE HIERARCHY
OF CREATIVITY

June Freeman

SEWING AS A WOMAN'S ART

The difference between craft and art, together
with the achievement and value of women's group
craftwork, are points taken up here by June
Freeman. She suggests the need for new critical
approaches to quilting, those which will not divorce
the aesthetic from the function. June is a sociologist
with a special interest in women's crafts; she has
organised exhibitions of quilting and knitting and is
currently working on cultural labelling and the
social order.

If we know something of the background to the art we
look at, its meaning comes across more fully and can stir us more deeply.
It's with this in mind that I want to write about quilting and its allied arts.

Today it is hard to realise how central sewing was to women's lives in
the past. Though sewing skills were undoubtedly necessary for comfortable
living, sewing was seen as so essentially womanly that it was taught
intensively from a very early age. Girls were often plying a needle by the
time they were three. This certainly helped to keep a woman's mind
narrow and her ideas unadventurous, so helping to ensure she knew her
place. But if sewing meant drudgery and oppression it also represented
much more. Sewing is the only lasting material thing many women have
left behind them. It is the voice of a huge section of the population who
do not feature in history books and who are otherwise silent. As an
American woman put it around 1900:

> I've been a hard worker all my life, but 'most all my work has
> been the kind that 'perishes with the usin'', as the Bible says.
> That's the discouragin' thing about a woman's work ... if a
> woman was to see all the dishes that she had to wash before
> she died, piled up before her in one pile, she'd lie down and
> die right then and there. I've always had the name o' bein' a
> good housekeeper, but when I'm dead and gone there ain't
> nobody goin' to think o' the floors I've swept, and the tables
> I've scrubbed, and the old clothes I've patched, and the stockin's
> I've darned ... But when one of my grandchildren or
> great-grandchildren sees one o' these quilts, they'll think about
> Aunt Jane, and, wherever I am, I'll know I ain't forgotten.[1]

Sewing, then, is the major means by which women in the past expressed themselves imaginatively. This gives quilting, patchwork and appliqué a special interest.

The best examples of quilting deserve, I believe, the same kind of attention that has been lavished on the work of such artists as William Morris and Charles Rennie Mackintosh. What strikes one forcibly about so many quilts is the artistic assurance of their makers' handling of colour, pattern and texture. The social and economic climate in which women

Mrs Lough, a Durham quilter

quilted, however, not only affected the appearance of the works but how it is appropriate to think about them. Most quilters remain anonymous. And when quilts are signed, indicating a proper pride on the part of the maker, the names mean little to us. For these women lived, with few exceptions, outside the world of high culture which is where the means of establishing artists' names beyond parochial and family circles have been developed. Both the comfortably off and the poor made largely for their homes and families. Even where they worked commercially and sold to the rich, as in the 1760s and 1920s and '30s, being predominantly women and working-class ensured that, even when their names were recorded, they remained effectively anonymous.

Muriel Rose, an energetic and appreciative art lover, organised the commissioning and sale of North Country and Welsh quilts during the 1930s. In her order books the buyers often have familiar names. Lady Diana Cooper bought from her. Few, however, would recognise the names of the quilters. Durham quilt clubs were another source of commercial quilting for a humbler clientele. These clubs usually had about twenty members, who each made small weekly payments to the woman who ran the club. In return she gradually, over a two-year period, furnished each of them with a quilt. From such clubs came hundreds of quilts by women whose names are already mostly forgotten and often never recorded. Not only did these women live in a world in which there were no outlets for publicising one's art beyond the immediate vicinity, but the idea of doing so would have almost certainly been foreign and embarrassing to many of them. A certain level of social confidence is required before a demand for recognition of personal achievement is made.

The anonymity of so much quilting means that it is impossible to bring together one woman's work and trace the development of individual skills and interests, as one might Morris's. An alternative approach must be used. As the anonymity of the work forces a reappraisal of critical approach, it is also central to an understanding of quilting that much of the work was done under conditions of considerable artistic constraint. In terms of design these artists did not stray outside the bounds of what was considered the proper domain of women. Fruit and flowers abound in quilting patterns. And in 1937 Elizabeth Hake recalled a West Country woman who remembered both grandmother and mother coming home with sprays of oak leaves, ivy, clover and thistle to study in the evenings as they planned their quilting patterns. Today a Northumberland woman can still recall how ideas for quilting were drawn from nature:

> on the coastline they had designs pertaining to the sea. Seaweed and shells. Very nice designs these were, belonging to Seahouses down to Amble ... the designs we had near the hills ... were all flowers and foliage and feathers.[2]

It was frequently considered unseemly for a woman to paint large-sized pictures. Impropriety was avoided, however, when the canvas was a quilt. Bedcovers as items of domestic utility could be designed without a loss of womanhood! Women who quilted generally accepted the constraints imposed by what their world considered seemly for a woman. Despite this they produced work of artistic quality.

But by the beginning of the twentieth century, certain middle-class British women had come to have considerable leisure, and some late nineteenth-century patchwork fashions reflect the need to be busy. We find a questionable tendency to see the amount of time spent on a piece of work as, of itself, an indicator of artistic merit. Here, social constraint may be seen as stifling women's creativity. Another constraint has also dogged many women in their quilting. Well-to-do women had rich remnants, and could also afford to buy additional material. By contrast, quilting among poor women was a scrap art. Yet what impresses so often in quilts made from scraps is the quality of colour and design in the finished product. It speaks of much thought and skill having gone into the planning.

Quilting then was frequently done under artistic and economically straitened circumstances by workers whose names are now forgotten. This does not mean, as sometimes seems to be supposed, that these women resolved their problems of design unconsciously.[3] Behind the confident artistry of many finished quilts lie intense and self-conscious struggles. As one woman put it, 'I keep figuring and working with my materials and thinking about my colours a long time before it feels right.'[4] There is also the story told by Muriel Rose of Emiah Jones, a Welsh quilter of the 1930s. Having decided on the main outline of a quilt design, Emiah Jones struggled all evening, without success, with one of the lesser parts of the pattern. In the middle of the night, however, she suddenly saw the answer to her difficulties. Sitting up in bed, she lit a candle and quickly drew the tricky part on the wallpaper, thus ensuring that it could be accurately transferred to the quilt-top in the morning.

A consideration of quilting as an art form raises questions about our approach to art generally. While women worked alone and produced quilts of great beauty, they readily got together to produce co-operative work at quilting bees. And the utilitarian purpose of quilts was always of central importance. Today, quilts are frequently displayed like modern easel paintings, neatly spaced on gallery walls. Their utilitarian purpose and frequent similarities of design are ignored. Attention focuses instead on the argument that they display some of the same properties as are found in the works of certain highly acclaimed abstract artists (Jonathan Holstein's writing on quilts offers a vivid example of this kind of approach). But it is doubtful if we do quilts justice unless we incorporate into our appreciation of them a recognition of their purpose and the nature of their design and making. Many kinds of Western art – theatre, film, dance and architecture – are necessarily the product of joint enterprise. But efforts are usually

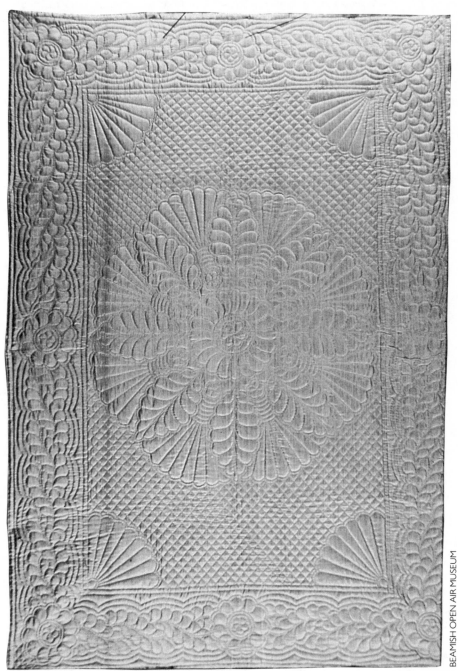

A North Country quilt from the early twentieth century

made to establish the greater importance of certain members of the enterprise, and often the supreme importance of one. It would seem plausible, however, that a group of women working together on a number of quilts would develop opinions about the design, which they expressed and discussed as a group. Further information about this would be invaluable. Are those quilts which display most satisfactorily a coherence in composition and the use of colour overwhelmingly the idea of a single woman? If not, how did groups of women plan a quilt?

The habit of so much group work had, I believe, an effect on the planning and execution of individually worked pieces. It encouraged an artistic style based on the constant modification and adaptation of tried and shared patterns. Though the creative woman gave her work an individual stamp, quilts reflected a communal design tradition. This deserves greater attention from the art world for what it can tell us about alternative routes to artistic achievement in latter-day Western society. Mrs Little of Northumberland has described her thoughts about artistic expression:

> Of course a lot of the patterns were very similar. But, let's face it, each worker is an individual and you may use the same template but everybody gets a very different effect. I mean I probably did a lot of things other people thought were not the done thing at all. But I got the result I wanted, and after all it was for my own satisfaction, wasn't it?[5]

Such an approach is very different in spirit from that of much of our art today. In fields like easel painting, where co-operation is not necessary to production, individual self-expression has been lauded.[6] This tendency has been strengthened by the intellectual concern in the world of high art with technical innovation, leading to a heavy emphasis on the new and different. And a recognisable personal style has now become the basis of an artist's saleability.[7] Yet, in terms of outcome, quilts, produced in a very different art world, are not in any way inferior to other art work more obviously individual in conception and technique.

Quilt clubs flourished, it would seem, because they met certain *social* needs for women. Men have found or created social groups for themselves, often as a by-product of their work. Women were, and are, often caught in the home, and more isolated than men. A jealous male world has also traditionally circumscribed women's freedom. But women, without offending male jealousy, could get together to quilt, gossip, eat and generally have fun. A member of a north country W.I. quilting group in the 1930s remembers:

> We always used to meet about two o'clock and hope to work till four, then stop and have a cup of tea. And we used to make scones, our own scones, and a sandwich cake or something, and we would share it out. We used to enjoy it. All the tales that were told over the quilting frame. Well, you could imagine.

> Everything was discussed! It was really entertainment making quilts...[8]

The need for human contact could thus be met through art. But quilting served a variety of other needs too: many stories have been told about how it met a woman's yearning for colour and beauty:

> I was dreaming of having all kinds of pretty things in my home after I married. Well, I found out right quick that livin' on a farm, what with all the chores that had to be done, a person didn't have a whole lot of time for makin' pretty things. But let me tell you, I got it all worked out with a little thinking. I had to drive one of them big wheat trucks during harvest ... when I had to wait for the men to load or unload the truck, I would just be piecin' on my quilt-top. They would all look into that truck and laugh. I'd laugh with 'em. That way I got my quilts done.[9]

Women have also recalled how the experience of death and loss has been channelled into gain through the design and work of quilting. Mavis FitzRandolph recounts, for example, how a Durham woman suffered a series of misfortunes, including sudden widowhood, so that she became 'very low in her mind' and apathetic. She decided, however, that she would start to quilt again. In the involvement of 'studying what to put on' the quilt, and then 'seeing the patterns form under her hand', she realised within herself a new energy and life. 'The quilting saved my mind,' she told Mrs FitzRandolph.[10]

But women who start quilting for personal and social reasons have found themselves becoming involved at a different level. One woman expressed this different level with the words, 'I'd rather quilt than eat when I'm hungry.'[11] The point is not whether this is true, but that it should seem appropriate to express one's feelings in this way. For here is a description of creative expression as a basic need of existence. What starts with personal need comes to benefit the art itself, and thus other people.

Women quilting now, while representing the continuation of a long sewing tradition, live in a world where the pattern of women's lives has changed in ways that are likely to be reflected in their art. A tradition of fine work was set up in the past by women without the aid of art school training, and there are women today keeping that tradition alive. They do not do this by copying old pieces. That would not only produce dead work but be contrary to the spirit of the tradition just described. They may start with an old pattern but they stamp it with their own individuality as the design and sewing develops. Women who have been formally trained have generally been encouraged to be more dramatically exper-imental in the handling of pattern and technique. Some seek more control over colour by rejecting commercial fabrics and dyeing their own, or by using spray paint. But no one approach dominates. The world would be

Susan Williamson, pieced cotton, early 1980s

SUSAN WILLIAMSON

more drab and sewing the poorer without the variety and adventure these women's work displays. Those who look for the expansion of artistic expression through the skilful handling of tried patterns can, I believe, find excitement and stimulus in some of these wide-ranging approaches. On the other hand, there is much for the formally trained to learn from the gifted amateur, whose work shows how a strong design tradition from the past can continue to afford fresh design possibilities today.

It is clear that deep feeling and hard thought have gone into the making of quilts, and behind the resolution of the finished products lie some prolonged tussles with design and colour. Yet quilts are neither solemn nor heavy and, although varied in style, their dominant feeling is of an exhilarating assurance. Insofar as they continue to communicate to us, quiltmakers will continue to benefit women generally by their display of unbroken spirit.

Kate Russell working on 'Threads' and 'Signs of Life', 1982

BARBARA BIRKS PHOTOGRAPHS

Kate Russell and Pennina Barnett

CRAFT AS ART

Kate Russell argues that it *is* necessary to separate the aesthetic from the function of a crafted object, in order to expand understanding of the craft aesthetic. Kate prefers to be labelled 'artist' because of the unwelcome connotations of the term 'craftswoman': 'It has the sound of the unthinking maker.' In this discussion with Pennina Barnett, Kate Russell speaks of her craftwork in tapestry and also describes how she has negotiated the education system as both student and tutor.

P.B.: Did you have a formal art education?

K.R.: I went to art college in the late '50s and was diagnosed as a graphic designer because my sketchbook was full of line drawings – a rather naîve diagnosis. But I left when I was nineteen without finishing the course, because I was pregnant. So I had the baby, and then got a job teaching design to hairdressers while my mother and mother-in-law looked after the baby. I've always done some kind of teaching, though usually part-time.

P.B.: Did you have much time to continue your artwork?

K.R.: I always kept up some drawing, usually views from the house, and I also drew the children of course, sitting on their potties where they couldn't move.

P.B.: Florence Nightingale wrote, 'Women are never supposed to have any occupation of sufficient importance not to be interrupted.'[1] I think that lack of continuous time is an important factor in preventing women from developing their own work.

K.R.: Yes that's true. I used to work in the evenings when the children had gone to bed because it was easier to carve out a space for myself then. But a lot of my creative expression in those years went into making clothes and toys for them. Later on, in 1970, I went back to college for two years and got a local diploma and then, more recently, I did a postgraduate year in textiles at Goldsmith's College in London. But my formal training is only relatively important. It's also significant that I've had three children, because the things I did for them also informed and enriched my art practice.

P.B.: Did you enjoy your early art education?

K.R.: Well, I've always regarded it as training, not education, because it didn't encourage any kind of questioning. But I enjoyed it from a social point of view; it was the first time I met people with whom I felt at ease. And I liked the practical side, using different materials, learning skills, yet – I also felt uncomfortable with it, I felt that something wasn't right, didn't jell. So most of my ideas have come from that feeling of discomfort.

P.B.: What was it that you felt so uncomfortable about?

K.R.: I couldn't express it at the time, and certainly not in these terms. But all the things I liked – cave paintings, African textiles, Greek vases – weren't considered 'mainstream' or part of art history, but as curios, as inspiration for the 'real thing', like the African masks that fascinated Picasso. My clearest memories from that time are of doodling from a book on Mimbres pottery [eleventh- and twelfth-century Amerindian pottery from New Mexico] and on another occasion from Greek vases, and being reprimanded for 'working outside my place and time'. The images I was drawn to, instinctively and for my own development, were denied by my instructors. So I just thought I was a misfit and a poor artist. I'm still more drawn to those kinds of things than to contemporary art, and trying to understand that connection is central to my work and to my teaching.

P.B.: From your recent experience as a student, and also as a tutor, would you say that those distinctions between 'fine' art and 'decorative' art still pervade art education? Are there noticeably different attitudes towards art and craft within art colleges?

K.R.: In every art college I've taught at there's still a hard core of Bohemianism – the romantic view of the artist – how can I put it without being incredibly insulting?

P.B.: Say what you mean!

K.R.: I've heard it said to students that they should 'take that wool off the frame and put a canvas on it'. That exemplifies a prevalent attitude towards craft, particularly to women's activities. Anything to do with fabric is derisively called 'knitting', with the inference of knitting circles, women's gossiping circles – in other words, triviality, domesticity, non-seriousness.

P.B.: How can that be combated?

K.R.: I'm not sure about combating, more like expanding what already happens on the course, to make space for other activities. There's too much emphasis on the conceptual in art education on the *idea* as the main source of creativity. I like the model of other functions or centres of intelligence – the intuitive, the emotional, the physical[2] – through which the individual can learn, and which can be stimulated through, for example, materials. We can know by examining and handling the physical stuff, we can learn its inner logic.

P.B.: Textiles have a tactile quality which painting, or more particularly drawing, doesn't have. Is that why you are so strongly drawn to them?

K.R.: Yes, your hands are more involved, and that seems to bring other senses into play. I don't mean that you don't use your brain when you make a woven image, rather that other parts of you are drawn into it as well. Painting and drawing are often thought of as requiring intellectual effort, and the crafts as more manually orientated, hence 'handicrafts'. But I think of hands as well as brain as being thinking. And I do think drawing is a more conceptual activity – in the arid sense of the word. It lacks something for me. I used to have a lot of doubts about drawing, it always seemed like a preparatory exercise.

P.B.: What made you start weaving?

K.R.: About four or five years ago I was doing an Open University degree course, and one of the aims of the Art and Technology unit was to present students who had no knowledge of art with a range of materials to work with, so that they wouldn't view art as just painting or drawing. As I'd had an art training, I wanted to find a medium that I'd not used before, to re-create that sense of excitement. I chose weaving, maybe because the materials were around the house, wools for knitting and so on. When I made that first image in wool there was something about the fact that it went right the way through, that it was an object that was being built, something tangible, that appealed to me. It was stronger than that, I just couldn't put it down. I liked the fact that a woven image is constructed from the bottom up. It's like building a wall, you can't build it from the top or the middle. I got a feeling of rightness from making that first piece, and it seemed to strike a chord with other people too, so many of them liked it.

P.B.: You've been exhibiting your work professionally for some time now. In that sense you've entered the public arena, the world of galleries, publications, funding bodies. You must have been drawn inevitably into the art/craft discourse. So how do *you* see your work?

K.R.: There are two strands: there's the speculative, more experimental side – the tapestries – which I think I'd have to call 'art', then there is the more decorative, functional work, like rugs and blankets, which I make to commission for a particular person or place. These are more directly influenced by indigenous textiles, like Navajo blankets... Nevertheless, I think I would say I'm an artist.

P.B.: Why?

K.R.: Because of the connotations of being called a craftswoman. It has the sound of the unthinking maker, even though I don't think that good craft is made unthinkingly.

P.B.: In a way you're accepting the status quo by using the most prestigious label. You even differentiate between your own experimental pieces and what you call the decorative, functional ones. You don't allow the work to stand up for itself, on its own merit.

K.R.: What I'm saying is that the work *cannot* stand up for itself in our society – rugs are walked on, metaphorically as well as literally. In a different society, in a different context, I could thoroughly enjoy working with the endless variations of colour and shape within a limited form. But in this culture and in this time, I also want to comment on the current devaluation of decorative work. In art criticism, especially in art colleges, 'decorative' is still used as an insult. So I'm trying to find a form where the most effective visual riposte can be made – a statement for the significance of decoration.

P.B.: I agree with you that decoration is still regarded as superficial, an adjunct. But what do you see as its significance?

K.R.: The more I've travelled and watched people making – women floor-painting in India, for instance – the more I believe it's short-sighted to dismiss decoration as something superficial or inferior. Pattern and decoration can be 'read' in many different ways; the signs, symbols and units of patterns have as interesting and varied a history and iconography as any other art form. In Indian aesthetics, for example, pure decoration without reference to narrative or symbolic meaning is considered to be a high form. The raga, a musical form, has as its first section pattern-making devoid of any function. The notes of a particular piece are chosen and then played with enough silence between them that you know what each note sounds like – just as you would lay out colours on a palette, so that you can see what you are working with. Then arrangements of infinite variety are played; notes are shortened, lengthened, heightened, played on different instruments, juxtaposed in endless sequences, and put together to delight the ear.[3] It makes me think of a kaleidoscope, and the way in which it shuffles and re-shuffles the same elements and colours, yet each time a new image is produced. As I see it, the rhythms of daily life, the kinds of things you do every day, like getting up, cooking, eating, the seasons and the yearly cycle, all make up some kind of pattern; although each day may have the same elements in it, they are arranged in a different order. And this is reflected in design and decoration, especially in more traditional cultures.

P.B.: Can you give me some examples?

K.R.: Yes, the imagery in eighteenth- and nineteenth-century pieced and patchwork quilts reflects elements of everyday life at the time, with designs like 'ploughed field', 'log-cabin' or 'sunburst', and the patchwork technique itself offers infinite variations on each design. Another example is the face painting of the Caduveo tribe of Southern Brazil, where there is also a relationship between the very process of pattern-making and social patterning. Levi-Strauss made a study of them in the mid-1930s and he describes how the women regularly painted each other's faces with intricate patterns – not from a pre-set formula, but improvising within the limits of a traditionally defined range of motifs and themes. These motifs expressed rank differences, nobility privileges and degrees of prestige, so their decorative art validated and interpreted the hierarchical structure of the tribe. Incidentally, Levi-Strauss collected over four hundred drawings of face painting from the Caduveo, and he claimed that no two were alike.[4] But decoration has all sorts of functions: in certain parts of West Africa the indigenous strip-woven cloth is thought to impart strength, fertility and protection to the wearer, and it's a crucial part of ceremony and ritual, especially in the wrapping of the dead. There are also traditional patterns for weddings, even a particular sequence for sewing together the different patterned strips, and apparently in some areas it's possible to tell which village people come from by the pattern in the cloth they are wearing.

P.B.: That used to be true of fishermen's ganseys. Many of the fishing villages on the Northumberland coast had their own distinctive pattern and decoration which incorporated motifs of coastal life, and it was from these patterns that washed-up bodies could be identified after a wreck.

K.R.: Yes, there are lots of examples nearer home: there are tartans identifying clan; heraldic shields expressing kinship and social privilege; playing cards with decorative King, Queen and Jack members; there are chess pieces, emblems, flags and religious symbols like the Star of David or the Cross . . . the list is endless.

P.B.: You mentioned that you wanted to make some sort of visual statement about the significance of decoration. The 'Fragments' series of tapestries which you were working on at Goldsmith's College seems to share some of the concerns of the '50s painters with mark making. Can you explain how that connects with your ideas about decoration?

K.R.: Yes. There's a connection between early letter forms, signs or marks if you like, and natural forms or patterns. Take the spiral: there it is in shells, fir cones, in the way water goes down a hole, and this same form is found all over the world, at different times, in early letter forms. It is regarded as a symbol of growth, what Jung would call an archetypal image. My views about decoration are influenced by the idea that there's a way of communicating through colours, shapes and symbols, without using words. You can see it in the way people choose which clothes to wear together, or in the complex inter-relationship of objects and coloured surfaces in any front room.

P.B.: The marks in those tapestries are almost hieroglyphic. Do they carry meanings?

K.R.: It's a bit tricky. Although I didn't intend to mystify, the idea is of a complex overlayering of meanings. There are at least two kinds of definable marks. Some are symbols that come more directly from natural forms and others are more obviously letter forms, Egyptian, Chinese, Arabic. To express the difference, some are actually bound into the construction of the piece, while others are literally overlaid by the thread travelling across the fabric.

P.B.: They're not immediately recognisable as letters or numbers. They seem fragmented, as if breaking down language.

K.R.: That body of work was influenced by reading the structuralists – Levi-Strauss, Saussure, Barthes – and came out of an interest in semiology, language as signs; the thesis that written marks making up a word (or sound) have no meaning in themselves, but are just a series of shapes or letters. They acquire their significance (or become 'signs') through the meanings that we assign to them, so that they come to represent ideas or concepts. Language, far from being neutral or objective, actually embodies the ideas and values of a people. My interest here is the commonality of all language when you take it back to its roots, as you take it apart... One of the most important insights I got from the structuralists was the value of looking at a structure (say a social structure) from the inside. For example, if you wanted to explain the seemingly odd customs practised by another culture, you couldn't really do it by making judgements based on the values of your own culture. It makes more sense to try and look at the customs in terms of that culture itself – its social conventions and behaviour, its history, its geography. Because all the things we take for granted – like language, cooking, table manners, dress and decoration – are external expressions of cultural values. If we look closely at these things we might be able to identify the underlying system of belief and, conversely, the underlying structure might help us to explain 'surface' events. So, to answer your question, yes! The ideas I was thinking about when I made those tapestries were to do with breaking down the constructs ('de-construction') and revealing the structure.

P.B.: Given this context, is the weaving process itself of particular significance?

K.R.: Well there's also a metaphysical level. The line or thread of life which moves through time and comes across different elements is acted upon and formed by experience; the threads which are brought together to form the fabric, and what is left out – the gaps, the spaces – this process is analogous to a way of looking at the unconscious.[5] These are the qualities I'm looking for in the way the pieces are woven.

P.B.: Can you describe that physically, in terms of the tapestries themselves?

K.R.: Although I start off with quite a structured idea, it is informed, modified, helped or hindered by the medium itself. Accident and experience are built into the process. I use different thicknesses of warp, or different materials with varying tensile strengths; some are smooth, fine and soft, others are resilient. So that when the weft thread comes across the warp, it reacts in different ways. In my very recent work the imagery is more personal and Mary Daly's positive reclaiming of language for women also figures, because her writing has validated and confirmed so many of my own ideas.

P.B.: In what way?

K.R.: I've mentioned my interest in taking language apart, discovering its roots and looking at the meanings we assign to words. Well, Mary Daly traces the derivations of words and shows how their meanings have been lost or modified to accommodate changing values, particularly patriarchal or misogynist ones. She reconstructs language in a way that makes more sense for women, reinstating ancient meanings to some words, and

BEN RUSSELL

A detail from Kate Russell's 'Signs of Life . . . and Death', 1986

inventing new and positive ones for others. An example that particularly interests me – and I'm using it to work out some new ideas for a tapestry – is the word 'trivia', because it is so often used to describe decorative work and, in particular, women's work. Trivia comes from the Latin *trivium* meaning crossroads – *tri*, three, and *via*, way. Mary Daly points to the importance of crossroads as significant turning points in our lives having 'cosmic significance'. She explains that in the Middle Ages crossroads, especially the meeting of three roads, were believed to be places of 'preternatural visions and happenings'. This was connected to the ancient idea of the world being divided into three parts and to the fact that the goddesses Persephone and Diana (associated with regeneration and fertility) and Hecate (associated with witchcraft) were also said to be known as Trivia, goddess of the three realms of earth, sea and heaven. They were associated with such divine crossroads.[6] Observing how the relationship of women to any craft practice was invalidated by the change in meaning of this one word, from being associated with powerful goddesses, through witch*craft*, to 'flimsy', 'minor', 'insignificant' and 'ordinary', 'of the street' . . . I saw the whole history of the de-gradation of women, and the whole possibility of re-claiming and re-assigning meaning to such words in accordance with our life experience.

P.B.: What are the personal elements that you're bringing into the new work?

K.R.: Well, again, it is to do with de-construction but, as I've said, the references are more personal. I'm going through a process of looking at my life, the achievements and the mistakes, and identifying the things that are and have been strong. As a woman I realise that I've lived far too much to external demands and have constructed myself to other people's notions of me, which are unsatisfactory and imprisoning. So I'm unpicking them thread by thread, taking them apart and re-constructing my image of myself in a way that gives me more freedom. I'm beginning to see that the 'differences' that I felt with such discomfort when I was younger are okay, are in fact to be celebrated.

P.B.: You mean the fact of being a woman ... *and* an artist or craftswoman. Those things are usually seen as incompatible, or at least ambiguous, even more so if you're a mother as well. It's as if you have to blot out the years of child-rearing and not mention them in the 'catalogue notes' of the art world. Women have to compartmentalise their lives. Finding a positive way of expressing the 'differences' and putting them into art is a real problem for women.

K.R.: I can remember very clearly feeling that I only operated within roles. As mother, artist, teacher. With no distinct sense of myself as a cohesive individual. The process I've been talking about – recognising the 'differences' – is definitely something I want to put into the work. I began to be more conscious of it about three years ago, just after I'd separated from my husband. I found myself making anguished doodles which jogged a memory from art college days. So I rummaged through my old work and amazingly found what I was looking for, a drawing of a procession of keening women – crying and grieving – that I'd made from a Greek mourning vase. At the time I was simply looking at the pattern and shapes, yet at some subconscious level I must have known what it was because I was so drawn to it. Looking at it again I had the distinct feeling that I was picking up threads from where I left off twenty years before – connections with my childhood too ... I was living at the time in a small terraced house, very cramped after the more spacious 'matrimonial home', and was reminded of an even smaller back-to-back terrace, and of my mother who worked in a mill as a winder, showing me how to draw and how to make a weaver's knot ... and I feel I'm reclaiming my history, my past.

P.B.: How are you putting these things into your tapestries?

K.R.: In a practical sense a lot of the skills and ideas refer to my previous work as a calligrapher, illustrator, set designer, needlewoman. Much of my recent work was in black and white, and I used paper in the actual fabric of the tapestry, so that connects it with my drawing. The way I use colour is significant, and again it's many-layered. Red is the only real colour I'm using at the moment, and I suppose it is the colour most associated with passion, anger, blood – but it also has socialist connotations. And it refers to signs being 'read' in the 'Threads' piece, which actually has the word 'threads' woven into it; then there's also an acute, painful use of red, like a gash or a wound. I hate explaining it because it sounds so pretentious, and primarily it has to work visually. In the piece that I'm working on now, 'Signs of Life', the red is a heart, like in a playing card, so again it alludes to signs and symbolism. For example, in alchemy – the medieval science which sought to find a way of turning baser metals into gold, the symbol of illumination and salvation – the Rubedo stands for menstrual blood and the animus of woman, which is seen as heart-inspired.[7] In this new piece the Greek woman has re-appeared but where her heart should be there is an empty space, for below her, falling off the edge of the tapestry, is the fragmented red symbol, like a seal or a signature. But above her is the reconstructed heart, a symbol of woman, her courage, vitality and vision.

Moira Vincentelli

POTTERS OF THE 1920s
Contemporary Criticism

The mediated differences between art and craft, or even between 'high' craft and 'low' craft are examined here by Moira Vincentelli. She shows how contemporary comment in the 1920s distinguished particularly between the 'little' work of women and the 'serious' artefacts of men.

Women have long been associated with ceramic craft. If evidence from many third world societies is to be taken, they were probably among the first potters, firing pots as part of their domestic routine. In societies where the potter's art became a professional task it is more usual to find a male tradition, as in most of Europe. No doubt, however, wives and daughters were useful hands in many country potteries, and in industrial society women were again pulled into the workforce as paid employees, often working in adverse or unhealthy conditions. As decorators in the factories they used skills of precision and neatness to reproduce standard designs.

In the nineteenth century ceramic decoration was considered an ideal medium for women. It conformed to all the stereotypes of women's art. It was decorative, small-scale, had domestic associations and did not require a heavy intellectual or philosophical content such as history painting, still the highest goal of nineteenth-century painters. Women made their mark in this field: John Sparkes, head of Lambeth College of Art, describes the collaboration between the art colleges and the Royal Doulton factory and sings the praises of the decorators, who were mainly women. The other activities, however – modelling, throwing and firing – were all male tasks. Painting on ceramics even became a fashionable middle-class pastime as well as providing useful income for some women.[1]

The feminist movement of the late nineteenth century had brought women greater opportunities and, while for most women the choice was very clearly one of marriage or career, art training offered some possibility of manoeuvre. Artistic interests were positively encouraged in women, especially middle-class women. Although few chose the professional artist's career in its full sense, growing numbers of women saw art education as a means of enriching their lives and giving them scope for an activity beyond the domestic role. Craftwork was the most acceptable end of art activities for women and, being less prestigious, was perhaps easier to include within the domestic routine. Pottery, however, is not quite so convenient as embroidery. It was not traditionally practised in the home as it was too messy and required special equipment for firing, but painting on ready-fired biscuit ware was quite easily accommodated.

After the First World War many young women had to face the fact that they were unlikely to marry and that they would have to earn a living in some respectable way. The dearth of men also allowed more women through the net when previously they would have been eliminated by fierce male competition. The Studio magazine in the 1920s has far more examples of art by women than at any other period.

An advertisement in The Studio in 1928 by the Association of Homecraft Studios Ltd., a mail-order firm selling craft kits, is aimed very directly at women and is redolent of the ideologies of the period. Addressed to women's need to earn money and to occupy their time in a rewarding way, it is in the form of a conversation between two women. One says:

> 'As well as teaching me art and crafts, the Association has shown me also how to create demands for them ... I am tired of the endless round of dances and parties, and would like nothing better than to fill in my spare time decorating art novelties.'

The advertisement is at pains to point out that anyone (even women) can do it by following the instructions offered by the Association, and it makes a play of the trendiness of this new hobby: 'Art novelties are so much the rage just now'. It stresses that the work is 'easy and entertaining' and that there is 'no drudgery' connected with it. In the last part it suggests that a woman can have a studio (like a real artist) 'attractively decorated and furnished' with 'a soft diffusion of warmth filtering through several parchment-shaded lights' creating 'an atmosphere of cosiness and orig-inality'. The lady in the picture even wears an artist's smock. This patronising advertisement reveals how fashionable arty-craftiness had become.

Similar attitudes also come across in The Times review of the 16th Annual Englishwoman Exhibition in the Central Hall, London, in 1926. This was something much akin to a craft fair, containing stalls displaying embroidery, pottery, jewellery, leather goods, woodwork and garments. There were even demonstrations of weaving and spinning. At the opening Mrs Baldwin (the Prime Minister's wife) suggested that women had mani-fested such obvious abilities that it was a wonder they had not taken up watchmaking! She also suggested that ladies could start up a 'treasure tinker trade' repairing broken articles. In this way they could be 'useful to the community', she claimed. The male tradition of fine art does not have to justify itself to the community, but even when women produce crafts mostly associated with domestic settings they are encouraged to find even more ways that they can 'serve the community'.

The large number of female potters in the studio pottery movement after the war was due to several factors. First, art training and art activities were acceptable for women; secondly, crafts of all kinds were marketable – the taste for handmade objects seems in many ways to be the final impetus of the Arts and Crafts Movement; and thirdly, there was a shortage of men after the First World War both as potential husbands and within the workforce.

Up until then the strict divisions between fine art, applied art and manual work were upheld in the art college system. However, an article in *The Pottery Gazette* of 1916 entitled 'Pottery Training for Women' (presumably because fewer men were around to take the courses) describes the teaching at the School of Arts and Crafts at Camberwell and indicates that changes were taking place:

> The first process taught is 'throwing', well suited to the delicacy of a woman's hand ... she proceeds to learn the making of plaster of Paris moulds for casting ware. There is also a lathe on which grooving and carving are learnt.

Industrial biscuit fired blanks were still widely used for decorating and when students did handle clay it was more likely to be for modelling or small-scale sculpture.

Although many women tended to concentrate on the more traditional areas of ceramic decoration and modelling, a number were attracted to the challenge of studio ceramics in its full implications, and indeed played an influential role as writers and teachers. One was Dora Billington, head of the pottery department of the Central School of Arts and Crafts from 1926. Her book, *The Art of the Potter*, first published in 1939, ran to many editions. As an artist her work drew particularly on the European ceramic tradition rather than the oriental so fashionable in the 1920s. Denise Wren was another potter, writer and organiser who often worked in collaboration with her husband. An experimental approach to her work led to the use of simple strong shapes and unrefined materials. She was particularly knowledgeable on the technical aspects of kiln building for

ADRIANO VINCENTELLI

Left to right: pots by Katharine Pleydell-Bouverie, Norah Braden and Frances Richards. From the Ceramics Collection of the University College of Wales, Aberystwyth

which she developed a number of projects. Frances Richards is another potter about whom little is known, but she exhibited regularly during the period producing unpretentious, mainly hand-built wares, variously coloured, suggesting an interest in experimentation in glazes.

Katharine Pleydell-Bouverie is perhaps the best known of all the women studio potters of the period. After a brief training with Bernard Leach at St Ives and a short spell at the Central School she set up a wood-fired stoneware kiln at her family home in Coleshill. She was joined in 1928 by Norah Braden and they worked together for eight years producing beautifully subtle but simple pots glazed with plant and wood-ash glaze. Careful and methodical in their approach, they kept precise records and their results were recorded painstakingly. Their sober glazes range in colour from oatmeal to yellows, greens and browns and suggest the natural earth from which they derive. Although influenced by the oriental tradition, they avoided the more spectacular effects of oriental glazes and very distinctive oriental forms. Their output is quite distinguishable one from the other, yet there is a harmony of intention which links their work and singles it out from any other potters' of the period. These potters are among the leading figures of the studio pottery movement, highly respected for their seriousness and integrity, although the quiet dignity and subtlety of their work makes it very much potters' pottery. But even their output, which was accepted within the mainstream of studio pottery, did not escape adverse comment from The Times' critic who suggested that their pots were hard and unemotional, concluding: 'The whole exhibition gives the impression of soundness. Emotional awakening will come.'[2] It is doubtful that the reviewer would have said that of a male potter!

Katharine Pleydell-Bouverie and Norah Braden had the good fortune to be working within the framework of modernist studio pottery. So far their work has stood the test of time, but another whole branch of ceramic art which was widely practised in the period has disappeared from accounts of modern British pottery. It is characteristic of art-historical writing that certain aspects become enshrined in the orthodoxies. Ceramic modelling has been excluded. Studio pottery was made by men and some women; ceramic modelling was practised largely by women with a small minority of male practitioners. The patronage of ceramic modelling was also, I suspect, largely from women themselves but that is difficult to ascertain.

One of the most successful artists in ceramic modelling was Gwendolen Parnell. After an early career in portrait painting she turned to ceramics. Her first exhibited figure of Henry VIII was bought by Queen Mary and she had a popular following from that time onwards. She employed female assistants in her studio in Chelsea, the area in London where many studio potters lived and worked. Each figure was modelled separately and was therefore an individual piece of art work. Parnell was a lady who moved

easily in high society, and in later years when she designed figures for the
Royal Worcester Porcelain Company she was nicknamed 'The Duchess'.
Writing in 1973, J. V. G. Mallet suggests that her work is 'over-coy'.[3] Her
figures were invariably produced in sets – illustrating 'The Beggars' Opera',
the Russian Ballet or 'The School for Scandal' – and are detailed, colourfully
painted and full of movement and expression. They appealed to the taste
for British literature and traditions, extending from the wide popularity of
similar subjects in many Royal Academy exhibitions. The subject matter
being parallel to painting probably lent the work an additional cachet and,
of course, their uniqueness was an important consideration for the collector
and investor. A reviewer in *The Times* in 1924 made the point clearly but
predictably:

> The ornamental figures … have of course their attractions but
> there does not seem much point in reviving a kind of pottery
> which is valued chiefly for its associations.

He meant reviving the Chelsea pottery tradition, and he went on:

> From these works, though undoubtedly pretty and amusing,
> one turns to the *serious* pots by such *workers* as W. S. Murray,
> Leach, Wells and Miss Dora Lunn. (my italics)

Frivolity is not acceptable to the Modernist taste.

There seems to have been quite a number of female ceramicists based
in Chelsea in the period, also working in what might be considered revivals
or survivals of earlier traditions. Kate Kitching produced models of birds
and Madeline Raper made pottery cottages conjuring up all the delights
of the 'olde worlde' England with thatched roofs and roses round the
door, but again they are belittled as works of 'ingenuity rather than of art'.
Reproduction of oriental wares was serious, while reproduction of English
decorative china was intriguing but clearly a lesser matter.

So far I have mentioned models that are a continuation of traditional
European ceramic production, but the great popularity of modelling as
part of art college courses encouraged the development of more original
techniques. This branch of ceramic art must have appealed enormously
to young female art students. It was small-scale sculptural work and would
have attracted many women who would have been put off by the heavy
and even dirty work that sculpture might have involved. It presented also
a saleable kind of art well suited to the domestic interior.

Phoebe Stabler was one of those who specialised in modelled figures
but sometimes produced larger works for garden decoration. She had
her own kiln at Hammersmith in London but sold the reproduction rights
of certain pieces to various factories including Royal Doulton, Ashstead,
Worcester and Poole Pottery, where her husband Harold Stabler, a
designer with whom she undertook joint projects, was a director. Her
work was enormously popular, and was usually of figure subjects, especially
women and children, modelled in a broad manner consistent with contem-

ADRIANO VINCENTELLI

Left: Irene Browne's 'Mother and Child Hagar', 1922; right: Phoebe Stabler's 'The Bath Towel', 1916. From the Ceramics Collection of the University College of Wales, Aberystwyth

porary sculptural techniques, with brightly coloured and glazed detailing in delicate blues, greens, and pinks. Reading between the lines of a review in *The Studio* yearbook of 1915, one can however distinguish the characteristically patronising attitude so often applied to women's crafts:

> There is a solidity and a compactness which give them much *charm* in silhouette . . . These *little* works make a human and often humorous appeal that constitutes an *attractive* feature apart from the considerable artistic merits they possess. (my italics)

A number of other modellers preferred a less colourful surface.[4] Their works were usually quite small, between five and ten inches high, and glazed all over with one colour. The modelling is not normally highly realistic and there is a slight looseness to suggest handwork as opposed to mechanical production. In general the subjects chosen are remarkably consistent with the stereotypes of female taste: women, children, animals. They are rarely humorous, but tend to be more serious or even at times melancholic. The work by definition is representational but it reveals a diffidence about over-naturalistic emphasis, though not nearly enough for The Times' critic in 1929. Writing of Stella Crofts, one of the best known animal modellers, he says:

> The impression here is that Miss Crofts is rather too easily successful on the zoological side and would gain from some drilling in what is called 'abstract' composition – designing in shapes that have no illustrative meaning. To go forward she will have to go back a little and study basic rather than incidental forms and characters.

When she was praised by another reviewer in The Studio of 1924, her work was given masculine qualities:

> Crofts' delightfully humorous animal groups in glazed pottery are always virile and distinguished in conception and modelling. (my italics)

It is interesting to follow the way that this kind of ceramic modelling was recorded at the time. It had to be mentioned because it must have been one of the most popular and saleable forms of art ceramics exhibited in galleries, but it is invariably subtly disparaged, as in The Studio in 1923:

> These particular manifestations of the potter's art (animal and figure subjects) have perhaps received from students a degree of attention somewhat out of proportion to their value, but the results are undeniably attractive ...

The writer went on to advocate what he called a 'democratic' point of view and suggested that they should concentrate more on work for the home or for industry rather than create 'ornamental luxuries'. In a similar vein, a review in the same magazine in 1926 of the exhibition of the Central School of Arts and Crafts states:

> In the pottery section the craze for figure subjects seems to be on the wane. This is a good sign, as the attention given to objects destined to fulfil a practical purpose is more essential.

By the 1930s this kind of work largely disappeared from the pages of The Studio. In 1932 in the review of the annual exhibition of the Central School of Arts and Crafts, previously one of the centres for this activity, the emphasis changed. There even appear to be almost no women represented in that year's exhibition.

By 1920 it might be assumed that hand-painting on ceramics was rather an outdated mode for the artist potter, but there were a number of practitioners of whom Louise and Alfred Powell were the best known. They were leading figures in the Arts and Crafts Exhibition Society who showed regularly in London. So good was the market for their wares that they were employed by Wedgwood to train girls to paint their designs.

As designers and calligraphers they developed silver and lustre decorations incorporating plant and animal forms combined with lettering. However, despite his ideals and close collaboration with his wife, it is surprising how easily Alfred Powell falls into the trap of identifying what is good in pottery with maleness and what is poor with femaleness. Remembering the past with nostalgia he wrote in 1929:

> The master-potter worked with his men too, quickening their enthusiasm. Merchants used to come in person, from places like Liverpool, to see what was 'out' and go away with their baskets full . . .
>
> We must set our minds towards uncovering the love of beauty in work . . .
>
> Instead, we put *little girls* – susceptible to all the *usual delights of childhood*, to sit in factories day after day placing *little* dabs of green and red on printed patterns until they turn into automatons. Their *little* minds stiffen up to the dull work and do it professionally, but it is a real tragedy and a loss that pottery cannot afford. (my italics)

His training, of course, offered greater freedom.

Studio pottery afforded genuine opportunities to women to find a fulfilling and rewarding occupation and career. However, I would like to suggest that certain branches of pottery have become the orthodoxy – the equivalent of the great masterpieces – while others are seen as secondary and less significant, and it seems clear that again women are largely in the latter group. Contemporary criticism reveals a subtle rejection of the feminine preferences in favour of what was identified as the new modern style.

Bernard Leach, Shoji Hamada, William Staite Murray, Michael Cardew have long been considered the great figures of early studio pottery. Katharine Pleydell-Bouverie and Norah Braden are usually classed along with them. I am not trying to suggest that one group is better or worse than the other. Our taste has been educated in these doctrines and it is difficult to get away from them, but it has to be remembered that they were only one aspect of studio pottery as practised in the period. The abstract, intellectual and functional were consistently praised as against the decorative, realist and ornamental.

While William Staite Murray's work is complimented for its abstract qualities in 'consistency of form, colour, surface and added brush decoration with no naturalistic disturbance', Stella Crofts', it is claimed, would gain from some drilling in 'abstract composition' and designing in shapes that have 'no illustrative meaning'.

An exhibition of decorative pottery is criticised for its lack of sobriety and simplicity. There is too much decoration, too much 'shop window effect'. Stella Crofts is praised when she gains in 'sculptural' qualities and Gwendolen Parnell for having attained 'breadth and fluency'. To call

WANTED
WOMEN AND GIRLS
TO WORK AT HOME

Do You Want A Pleasant Way of Making Money in Your Spare Time At Home?

The Association of Homecrafts Studios now makes it possible for you to earn money in your own home in fascinating **Arts and Crafts.** Read our offer to provide TOOLS & MATERIALS. The demand for decorated art novelties is enormous, and is steadily increasing. There are BIG CASH PROFITS in Arts and Crafts for anyone who likes to try. This absorbing occupation is so fascinating that it could scarcely be called work at all. Imagine the pleasure in decorating quaint wooden novelties with brilliant harmonising colours, or in making up useful articles from Leather and modelling rich designs upon them. Think of making a Leather Bag, perhaps only a few hours' work, and realising a profit of 30/- or £2. YOU CAN DO IT—it is being done every day by others.

The Association of Homecrafts Studios is an organisation with members in every part of the World. Members conduct their own studios, and are taught Leather Craft, Pewter Work, Lampshade Making and Decorating, Wood Painting and Enamelling, Gesso, Batik and many other highly interesting and profitable crafts. Members are shown how to sell their wares to the large shops and also how to set up delightful and money-making Arts and Crafts Studios of their own.

MORE MEMBERS WANTED

The Association purchases the latest fashionable novelties and craft materials for its members in English and foreign markets. We want more members to enable us to buy supplies in still greater quantities, thereby reducing the cost at which novelties for decorating can be supplied to our associate workers. As a special inducement we are offering tools and materials FREE OF EXTRA CHARGE if you enrol at once.

NO TALENT NEEDED

You don't have to be able to originate designs in order to be successful. That is all done for you. The Association retains experienced artists who are constantly evolving new and original designs and colour schemes, which are furnished to members by means of full-size working diagrams and colour charts. Every design is drawn specially for the decoration of some particular article. You have only to trace the working drawings and use your colours according to the charts. These designs, which cannot be used by anyone outside the Association, will simplify your work immensely. You will love Arts and Crafts more and more each day as you progress. You can do this work. Hundreds of others are doing it already.

LEARN AT HOME

You can learn in your own home to decorate Art Novelties. The Association teaches new members by means of a specially prepared Correspondence Course of Lessons. You learn by practical methods. With the first lesson you begin doing work which you can readily sell. The instructions are so clear, and the working designs, which have only to be traced, make it all so easy, that you will find that you can produce beautifully decorated novelties almost immediately.

MORE ORDERS THAN THEY CAN HANDLE

Members are writing continually saying that they have more work than they can do. From all parts come reports of success.

ILLUSTRATED BOOK FREE

A Beautiful Book has been prepared which tells you how YOU, too, can make money in your spare time in Arts and Crafts. It is called "HOME CRAFTS." Let us send you a copy free, without obligation on your part.

WARNING

This special offer of Tools and Materials is intended for immediate applications. Write your name and address on the coupon below for full particular NOW.

> The Association of Homecrafts Studios, Ltd.
> 121 Greycoat Galleries, Greycoat Place,
> Dear Sirs,   LONDON, S.W.1
> Please send me your book,"Home Crafts,"
> and full information about the special offer
> you are now making. I enclose 3d. in
> stamps for postage, handling, etc.
> *Please Print in Block Capitals.*
>
> Name ....
>
> Address ....
> ....

CHRISTMAS GIFTS—The work of members—On view and for sale at 94 Petty France (next St. James' Park Underground Station), LONDON, S.W.1—*See What We Teach*

AD. XIX

An Association of Homecrafts Studios poster from the 1920s pottery sculpture clearly lends it the prestige of 'art', so Aline Ellis's animals 'do not pretend to be sculpture' but remain true to the description 'models from life'. The notion of the 'artist as researcher' is praised while it was important at all costs to avoid the 'bazaar crafts'.

Studio pottery provided a space for women to develop their creative talents as potters, as painters, as experimenters testing the chemical properties and effects of different clays and glaze mixtures, as sculptors modelling clay and as businesswomen. Despite the undoubted opportunities, however, women must also have found themselves constrained by the dictates of male values and male standards of taste. The branches of the potter's art that obviously appealed to many women in the 1920s have been set aside in more recent accounts of the period in favour of the branches of studio pottery that appear to be more forward-looking and parallel with the contemporary modernist art. Current art-historical accounts of painting in the 1920s have begun to give more weight to the realism in fact widely practised in those years but overlooked when abstract art seemed the only relevant kind of art. A similar bias seems to have been at work in ceramic history, with particular consequences for women's role within it.

Pauline Barrie working in her studio

NICK MORRIS

Pauline Barrie

REFUGE IN ENAMEL
From fine art to hard craft

Pauline Barrie has found refuge from the world of
fine art education in the art of enamelling. She lives in
Kingston, Surrey, and works as organiser of the
Women Artists' Slide Library, an institution she
was instrumental in founding.

My problem has been that I've always felt that I'd got
to wherever I was by the skin of my teeth; it's seemed that hanging in
there was a real question of survival. It's a hang-up in part due to geography
– it's difficult to place the manners and meanings of different locations.
Coming down from Cumbria to London at twenty, I felt like an innocent
mistakenly stowed aboard a discriminating institution of mysterious quality.
I was desperate to grasp the rules I couldn't find, feel the hidden touchstone,
come out as one of the boys, even. At art college with all male tutors (I
wasn't taught by a woman artist/tutor till my last year), I too wanted those
favours bestowed on the few, the young heroes in whom the tutors saw
themselves re-born; I too wanted the extra six pots of Titanium oil paint.
But I got nowhere near the extra paint; I was labelled 'unteachable' and
given 0 per cent for most things. But the deviant niche fuelled my energy.
Still desperate to achieve, I competed for, and won, scholarships, prizes,
commissions; I exhibited, I sold, I even finished up with a first-class degree
and a postgraduate place, despite them all. But I bitterly resent all the
fighting I had to do, all the soul-searching to find out what was wrong with
me that I didn't fit in – such a waste of time and energy, and all I finished
up doing was painting for a male art world. It had little to do with me,
which is why I've since been involved with enamelling. The art world
pressures have been more distant from me in the enamelling workshop
than they were in the painting studio. So after six years of college and
competition, when I was back on my own and trying to sort it all out, it
was in enamel that I worked to find my own language.
    I first worked with glass at college in Lancaster. Even there I'd felt that
my acceptance had been by a hair's breadth, because everyone (family,
headmaster, college principal) thought that an art course was inappropriate
for a girl, especially one with academic 'A' levels. The course I followed
at Lancaster was industrial-based with much concentration on technique.

I studied industrial ceramics and three-dimensional design, metalwork and woodwork, photography and silkscreen – all the things I'd wanted at school and had been prevented from doing as a result of academic streaming. I worked so hard there, I took voluntary night classes in the metal workshop and also with the painters and decorators. Most of the work was real craft training; in the painting and decorating we made up mock doors and we produced pub signs, we learnt about staining and rag-technique – none of it anything to do with slopping on emulsion with a roller. The wood workshop was wonderful; the college had taken on a redundant craftsperson and a technician from a local company and they knew so much and crammed us as full as we could take. They were so excited to have students wanting to learn from them, that all of our enthusiasm was generated. And there was no obvious gender prejudice at Lancaster. At art college in London later, the technician there thought a woman would need an instant hysterectomy from carrying three bits of two-by-one; he wouldn't believe that I knew how to saw the stuff, let alone sharpen the saw.

I got involved in stained glass at Lancaster. I think my initial attraction for it came from childhood years of compulsory choir practice. Lancaster had been a centre for industrial stained glass, though when I was at college that was dying. I did a project with the last glass company in the city; it was a design for shop-fronts, and when I visited the company they gave me a lot of samples to take away. I used those samples for a long time in my artwork. When I moved to London and went to Kingston Art College, one of the first pieces I did was to do with ceremony and church symbolism, and I used stained glass in that. In my second year at Lancaster I painted a lot and decided to concentrate on that. But I chose Kingston Art College because it had a kiln and I knew that I wanted to work with glass as well. So my main subject for three years as an undergraduate was painting, and enamelling the subsidiary; because of that, enamelling assessments were not so crucial and in the workshop I didn't feel driven to be (and make) what I couldn't achieve anyhow, by virtue of my femininity.

'Femininity' was a problem anyhow for me at this stage. I couldn't identify with the projected personae of so many women, nor conform to what was expected of me by men. It had always seemed to me that the most interesting things in life were done by men, and I wanted to do them too. It was my father who had encouraged me to think and to study; there was no woman I wanted to emulate. But I had been brought up in this very traditional northern family; there was me, and three brothers, and I was the second slave of that family – it was a position I had thought was natural, but came to resent. I gave my mother hell for a long time because I devalued her nurturing role; I was reaching for a different mode of being. It took me a very long time to appreciate my own femaleness and, as a result, that of other women. But as a student in London from

1972, I joined the Artists' Union and became a member of the Women Artists' Collective; it was that experience which began the change in me. It enabled me to identify my problems as originating outside myself, in my environment, and in the socialisation processes we all go through. Eventually, I was able to come to terms with myself, with other women and with our gender.

Anyway, after those six years of college it took me two years to recover, to stop chasing 'success' and 'acceptance' from men, and to begin to find my own work. I had been created as 'other' than artist by those art college institutions, and being female remained a problem after college too. The assistant or technician takes on more than the discipleship of the student; he is the re-creation in the artist's own image. Being 'other' than male hardens into 'other' than artist, and 'other' than craftsman. Enamelling is clothed in male mystique because of the very complicated and potentially dangerous techniques involved – the chemicals, the firings, and so on; the mystique is helped by the twentieth-century development of enamelling on sheet steel. There are a lot of secrets in the workshop traditions, secrets passed from master to student, and most fully through initiation by assistantship. Being uninitiated by virtue of femininity therefore remained a problem but, by this time, through feminist consciousness, the gender problem didn't penetrate my mind, it just touched my politics. But I had been very lucky indeed to have been initially trained in industrial crafts. It enabled me to jump some of the gender hurdles, even at Kingston, because I already knew I could learn the basics of a craft, say metalwork, alongside young males. And finally, enamelling does feel less contaminated by twentieth-century art world macho.

So much of my work in the last eight or nine years has been in enamel, and it's been an activity far from public discourse. It's all been about me. That enamel out there is about me inside; it's about me claiming an identity, knowing myself; me, a speaking person who is female. My involvement is the discovery of my own identity, finding my own images, and the dialogue is inward. I don't need, or want, public discourse; I don't need my work to be part of some ongoing aesthetic, even feminist aesthetic, discussion. Even though I know that my work is political, in that it uses 'female imagery' and could intervene in the phallic art world, I also know that it's not political in ways that most political artists see as useful. My work is private, painfully private, and I don't show much, only when the work finds a place for itself, is asked for. The content of the enamels seems so fragile, I don't want to lose sight of them. But the medium is strong. Enamel is composed of layers and layers of glass, all of them fired at very high temperatures. They'll last forever, my enamels. Save the worst, they're indestructible. My enamels will outlive me. That really gives me a voice, gives me strength. I, a woman, making work about being female, about cycles and circles, saying things that haven't been said before out there, and in a form that can't be destroyed – that will be public compensation for this private fragility.

Angela Hinton at work on stained glass in her Birmingham studio

PROFESSIONS TO CRAFTWORK

These three short pieces are from women who have deliberately abandoned stable professions in order to seek greater job satisfaction in craftwork.

Architecture to stained glass

ANGELA HINTON is single, lives alone, and enjoys independence in her work with stained glass. She first worked as an architectural assistant for a city urban renewal scheme, but left to gain independent job satisfaction.

For me, the trouble with architecture was the number of negotiations involved. I worked on an urban renewal scheme and was concerned with the renovation of old houses. Everything I did had to be vetted by several other people; I had no real control at all. And I was working with men all the time – not that I've anything against men, but women in building and architecture are thin on the ground, and dealing with all male building workers on site is very problematic. They find female authority very hard to take and believe it to be incompetent. It was the same with each new set of workers: every time, they would get me to climb up the scaffolding so they could wolf-whistle. With the need to negotiate at both ends of the process I was left with little creative satisfaction and no confidence. It was the same at college too. There were three women on my architecture course amongst forty men, and no women tutors. I think that all of us women felt the constant need to prove ourselves against the odds of variations on scaffold-climbing. The whole college experience knocked my confidence and I've only managed to regain it through practical work on site and, since then, through stained glass work.

I started working full-time in stained glass about three years ago. I'd come to enjoy the decorative aspect of glass that was nevertheless used functionally within building. The play of light is subtle – even on older, terraced houses where the glass work is usually of a low standard it individualises the separate dwellings. I took a short course to learn about the materials and tools and various stages in the process. It was a 'hobby' course, run by one of the few people left still taking regular classes because most of the old practitioners have died out; we now have to learn through doing. I spent the first year doing the learning, not for a living, then, by word of mouth, jobs began to come in, often through my contacts with architects. At first the work was mostly repairs to leaded lights and house windows. It's still very sporadic and I can live only at subsistence level, but I'm much happier than I was as an architect. I think I'm more comfortable dealing with inanimate objects and materials, and also having complete control of the whole process from design to finished article.

I find justifying my ideas very difficult and I'm hopeless at 'selling' myself, so they've always told me, and anyway I don't like doing it. But now I do feel I could cope with a craft centre perhaps, and I also need to break into new fields – church work for example. That's where the large studios make their money and there's a great deal of work, mostly conservation, which is totally different from what I've been doing, but I'd like to take it on now. The biggest piece I've tackled so far was about six feet by three and a half feet. It was a panel for a design studio in London for which I had a reasonably free hand, unbound by tradition, and enough money. They chose a design of irises from ten I suggested. I think it worked well, especially because I found exactly the right piece of glass for the subject. All stained glass is handmade, no piece is like another; and I found one that had varying intensities of colour across the sheet, suggesting the veins of an iris petal. Usually the designing I do is not so exciting because people have strong ideas about what they want and we have to negotiate from there. Working for a craft centre instead of to commission could give me more freedom in the design. That, with conservation work, would give me satisfying and above-subsistence living, and it's what I'm aiming for.

Academia to liberation

JEANETTE HONAN comes from a highly motivated teachers' family and was prevailed upon to follow the profession, finally teaching French at an American university. She came to England in 1968, gave up teaching and made jewellery at home, showing and selling her pieces through galleries. She describes how she developed her craft into a political activity.

Around 1977 a friend asked me to make her a pair of Women's Liberation earrings. It seemed a good idea, but an expensive one. Then together we thought about making them in bulk; the notion of earrings worn as badges took off. We designed models of the women's symbol and worked with a casting company. For the National Women's Liberation Conference in Birmingham I ordered four hundred castings in silver, and borrowed money to pay for them. I sold out in two days. In a way it's taken over; I advertise in *Spare Rib* and *Sanity* and work for mail order companies, and feminist bookshops sell the work. I have student help from Birmingham Polytechnic, otherwise I would spend every evening just polishing. I've made designs for the Peace Movement and for the Campaign for Nuclear Disarmament, and I still make non-political jewellery in slack periods. But I don't want to make very expensive things any more; I normally work in gold only for women who are allergic to silver.

I also work in the jewellery quarter of Birmingham. It's a part-time job, and it has given me a lot of contacts and information, and put me in touch with a lot of working women. They are often highly skilled, and yet their work is undervalued as salaries are traditionally low there. Firms are run on a patriarchal basis and unions are almost non-existent. I know a wonderful woman in her seventies who started training as a very young girl; she is now one of the very few who can repair intricate Victorian and Georgian jewellery. Her work reaches the high street jeweller or the fashionable antique dealer at a price she would not recognise and yet, talking to her, I find she often apologises for the very little money she charges. Women still accept undervaluation of their work, in craft fairs or in sweat shops. It makes nonsense of all our lives. Just because quilting, for example, is part of our women's tradition should not mean we have to apologise for selling it.

Jeanette Honan, jeweller, with the Women's Liberation earrings she designs and makes in Birmingham

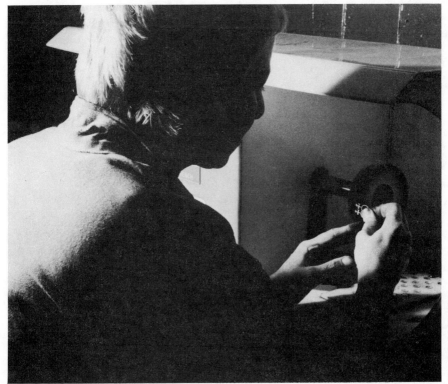

SOLVEIG JORGENSEN

Teaching to jewellery-making

NESTA PUGH

As a teacher I was pushed up the rungs of a career ladder I didn't believe
in, forced to curtail my creative activities in order to fit in with timetables
and general bureaucratic structures, so I walked out. I began part-time
classes and squared up to the poverty it entailed. As a self-employed
person I now work harder, but with less sense of grudge. Life is scarier; I
value both my money and my time more than I did, but I miss the
comradeship and active trade unionism I shared before. I've found greater
generosity of spirit and purse amongst self-employed people, but also
greater selfishness.

I make silver and gold jewellery, and I silversmith small items, boxes
and enamelled pieces. Before I had a baby, four months ago, my work
dominated other commitments. It's very labour intensive, so my politics
and my recreation had to find outlet at the fairs and women's events I
attended to sell my work. Women's Liberation jewellery, which I make,
implies a shared philosophy; discussions and ideas exchanged whilst selling
and showing work have been an experience of collective consciousness.
I think it has been possible for me, because I'm self-employed, to organise
in a womanly way, to break out of the formal codes of business language,
and to talk to people as human beings. This in turn has affected my
jewellery, even more now that I am a mother; my feelings towards women
have been strengthened, and I think my designs will show it.

Cindy Harris

AGAINST THE GRAIN
Learning a man's craft

Cindy Harris tells of her struggle to gain confidence
in the building trade crafts, while bringing up two
children. She now works as a carpenter, alone or
with others on group roofing projects, and she also
job-shares as an area caretaker.

The main area of my work is carpentry, but over the
years I've picked up other skills – plumbing, electrical work, bricklaying. I
started with a City and Guilds course in carpentry. It was important for
me then that I'd known another woman who'd done that particular course:
without that example I'd not have had the courage to do it. I was very
under-confident and couldn't see myself as a practical, manual worker at
all. It was in a male-dominated building department; I was the only woman
student and I was treated with contempt, and sometimes amusement, but
most often just ignored, and it was mostly horrible. I was a single parent
with two children and all my energy went into getting through that bloody
course, for two years.

Mine was a day-release course. I'd have liked to do a TOPS one because
you get paid for that and it takes only six months, and you get a free
tool-kit at the end of it. My having two small children prohibited that; I
could be out only part-time. My course consisted in one day and one
evening each week, which is why it took me two years. I was working as
a counsellor for the British Pregnancy Advisory Service and the money I
earned more-or-less covered my fees and expenses, together with our
living costs. So training for my Craft Certificate was very time-consuming,
just to get to the point where I felt able to pick up a hammer and knock
a nail in straight. I had so many lapses of confidence and motivation, and I
very nearly left in the second year. Training courses are not designed to
suit women's needs in terms of our domestic responsibilities, added to
which, for me, there was a whole problem of confidence about entering
a field where, by definition, men are the experts. There were no women
I could go to. It was difficult to maintain a belief in my ability even to finish.
I did accept that I had to learn from men – indeed, I'd first been attracted
to wood and to building things by watching men, a few, who had inspired
me to learn more and treated me as if I could. But the men at the building

college were hopeless; they just taught me because they had to. There's a terrible mystique involved in the building trades, to do with the fact that if it doesn't work, then my God, you're going to be electrocuted, flood the house out, or the wall's going to fall down! Even sympathetic men I know are quite conscious about perpetuating the fear. They know they're doing it and they'll laugh about it, but they still do it; only now I can be included in the joke because I'm almost one of them. But it is difficult for them to forgo the control their knowledge gives them.

After I'd finished the course I started very small bits of private work, although actually the first job I did was a fitted wardrobe which was a big job. I was hunking sheets of chipboard around and wondering what I was doing. Something also about doing a craft is the tools for it. They are very expensive and if you don't have the right ones it's tempting not to start the job at all. It's no good trying to cut a mortice with a blunt chisel or one that's the wrong size, nor plane a piece of wood without a decent vice. To begin with I didn't have a proper workshop: it was a shed at the bottom of the garden, and I had few tools. There's this problem with woodwork – being a bit like gardening or potting, it's relegated to the garden. Really, if it's integral to your daily life, like cooking in the kitchen or sleeping in the bedroom, then it makes sense to have a large, light, airy and accessible workroom.

A while later I got a job as an area caretaker. Caretaker projects work in conjunction with local authorities' urban renewal schemes in inner city areas. They are funded by inner city partnership and managed by local residents' associations. An area caretaker covers about half a dozen streets and can be called on to do all sorts of maintenance work for owner-occupiers and tenants. Mine is a job-share. We organise, for example, skips for rubbish removal; we can lend out tools, and we take on some large structural jobs, such as re-roofing. We have a big workshop; we've built our our own workbench and have a bandsaw and good tools. I started six years ago and my general building and maintenance skills have developed as I've gone along. Slowly and painfully I've gained 'fault diagnosis' capacity, essential to the job. Th experience has been very important over the years because I can recall how terrified of everything I once was, and I'm aware of my confidence now. That gives me a lot of job satisfaction, and ever-increasingly the work has become necessary for my mental and physical wellbeing.

Roofing has been one of the most satisfying tasks for me. It's given me confidence to work at heights on scaffolding, and it's fascinating to have the structure of the building revealed when the roof's off. Apart from the caretaking, I've also worked on roofs with groups of people from all over the country. Usually we've worked on old farm buildings – one of them was a Grade Two listed building which we re-roofed with stone slabs. When my own house needed a new roof, I'd got to the point where I could set up and co-ordinate the whole job, with various people turning

Cindy Harris at work on a roofing contract: she has worked on everything from a Grade Two listed building using stone slabs to re-roofing her own home

JULIAN HOWELL

up to work with me. I've also felt free to tackle large projects on my own house. I have completely re-wired and re-plumbed it, and done a loft conversion for which I provided flooring, ceiling and electricity to the roof-space, together with natural lighting sources – an opening window in the roof and a french window on to a roof platform/patio – and plastered the walls. I've felt confident enough to start out on these projects even though I haven't all the answers, and delays have ensued while I consulted 'experts', having made mistakes that had to be rectified. Lately I've developed an interest in designing what I make, mostly the furniture. I've designed a sofa, chair, bed-bases and fitted kitchen units. It's important for the woman as worker and consumer to question assumptions, such as the one about the kitchen being a small room at the back of the house. We need to work to change things to suit our needs. It can be done; my kitchen is at the front of the house in a large, well-lit room, the work units are where I want them for convenience, and the surfaces are at the height, and of material, that is most efficient for me. This has opened a whole new area to me, where designing and building go hand-in-hand. In two weeks I'm off to London to design and re-build a kitchen for a client, and I'm really looking forward to that.

One of the things about all the building crafts is the degree to which they have been undervalued. If you think back to the last century, or before, the crafts were dynamic. You went along and you did your five years of apprenticeship, or more, and you really learnt how to turn a bit of hardwood, or to make one of those beautiful panelled doors with huge mortices. Now, a woodworker can be somebody who just nails a hardboard panel on to a frame, for a door. I think that women building workers are in general more concerned with preserving traditional methods, tools and materials, than are men, although that's odd because it means our harking back to a past that isn't ours. It was a male preserve, and men had those lovely polished tools which we didn't understand and couldn't handle. And still women are brought up to believe that this whole area of work is outside their understanding. Many women still think they can't cope without a man, even with changing the fuse and basic house maintenance. It contributes to our feelings of powerlessness.

For a woman in the building trade the male tradition has other effects too – for example, I take even mild criticism very personally. A man would shrug it off, but I take it to heart because if you're a woman doing a job it's got to be bloody perfect; it can't just pass, you know, it has to be wonderful or it's no good at all. With the caretaking I do a lot of work outside and I have people I don't know informing me that I'm taking a man's job away from him. Many male building workers will just assume that they've got the right to come up and talk down to me. Being a woman out there seems to give everyone the right to patronise; I've even had them attempting to take my ladder away from me. And accepting help is fatal; they just take over. And we women, because we're under-confident, say things like, 'Oh well, I built this but it's not very good really.' We're always undervaluing ourselves.

It is politically important for women with building skills to maximise training opportunities for other women, and arrange for mutual support in an industry which is particularly male-dominated and sexist. There are national conferences and newsletters organised by Women and the Manual Trades which help to keep women in touch with each other and with what's happening in the industry. Recently I've become involved with the Women's Training Workshops in Birmingham: these run courses for women, taught by women, in computing, electronics, and building skills and crafts. Although employment opportunities remain very limited afterwards, it's nevertheless important for women to have access to this kind of training. I am now investigating the possibility of setting up a business to buy and renovate old houses, incorporating some of the more unusual features I've used in my own house.

June Statham

OF BIDDLES AND SPARS

June Statham worked for the Open University as a researcher and education consultant for eight years, then moved to North London where she lives in a shared house. She now divides her time between writing, roofing and thatching.

I've learnt not to say 'thatcher' when people ask me what I do, or at least not without explanations. There's the problem of the knee-jerk response that equates 'thatcher' with Conservative politics; looks of blank incomprehension; and the fact that I'm also a researcher and writer, and in our culture people are expected to specialise, rather than to attempt to bridge the gap between mental and manual work. But for me, it has been the combination of those two ways of working that has given me the greatest satisfaction and pleasure.

I started roofing several years ago, when I was working as an academic at a university. A network of people living in housing co-operatives, as I was at the time, used to get together to mend each other's roofs on a skill-sharing, self-help basis, and thatching grew out of that. It's a difficult craft to find a way into. There are no formal training courses, and the usual way of learning is to become an apprentice to a master thatcher, traditionally for four years. (Mistress thatchers are so rare as to be in practice non-existent.) I was lucky in knowing someone who thatched part-time and was prepared to teach me. I'm still learning.

One of the first things I learnt, which I think I'd always suspected, was that the reality of thatching is quite different from the romantic image of picturesque country cottages with roses rambling over the porch. A lot of the time it's hard, dirty, tiring work: eyes, lungs and hair filled with dust from stripping off the old thatch, hands blistered from struggling to twist the hazel sticks that hold the new straw in place, muscles aching from carrying endless bundles of straw and from climbing up and down ladders all day. When it's cold and wet and I've been up since 6 am, the knots won't pull tight and I can't find a rafter to nail to, then the frustration can feel, literally, like the last straw. But the compensations are many: the sun on my back as I work high on the ridge, the lovely sweep of the roof line over a window, the satisfying thud of the spars as they fix firmly into the old thatch beneath. I love the old words for the tools and materials: spars, biddles, leggats and sways – traditional names for a traditional craft. There's something particularly beautiful and satisfying about a newly laid thatched roof, a solid chunk of gold that's laid on almost straw by straw. It feels like a closer, more personal connection with the material than I have when covering a roof with slates or tiles. I experience that as replacing a hard shell over the roof, whereas thatching involves creating a roof out of something soft and organic, persuading a fragile, non-waterproof material to form a solid, waterproof covering. No hard edges, no power tools; a different, muddy kind of dirt. Over one ton of straw goes into an average-sized roof and each bundle is carried up, cut open, laid armful by armful and knocked into shape by hand or with a few wooden tools. It's a more deliberate, conscious shaping of the environment.

That ability to shape and control the environment has been for me the most important benefit of learning manual skills. It has subtly changed the way I look at the world. I notice houses a lot more now. I look at buildings and roofs to see how they are made, take in the shape and inter-relationship of built things, and am fascinated by the different materials and colours and textures. It makes me want to create things for myself, to shape some of the environment into forms I respond to – into particular kinds of spaces: patios and courtyards and curving low walls; brick and wood and thatch; climbing and trailing plants; stained glass and coloured light; archways, conservatories, changes of level. It's not that I think I could

June Statham with straw prepared and ready for thatching

JUNE STATHAM

The end result: a romantic image which belies the hard, dirty, tiring work which has gone into it

build any of the houses I see around me, but I somehow feel that I understand them more, or see them more. It's as though the material world no longer exists as huge constructed lumps that are just there, but is broken down into a series of processes that I can get to grips with even if I can't actually do them all.

There still is a difference in the way I approach crafts that traditionally have always been done by men. I don't remember ever having to learn the kind of 'feminine' crafts that I've done since I was a child – things like sewing, patchwork, appliqué and toymaking. They are a part of me that I rarely question. I can cut without patterns, visualise how something will look before I start, and I know that if I make a mistake the chances are I'll be able to put it right. I know how the parts fit together and how the various processes work. With thatching and roofing, on the other hand, I don't have that same confidence that if something goes wrong I'll find a way around it. The 'male' skills still feel external to myself, tacked on rather than something I've grown up around. Maybe it's a question of time, and experience. The attitudes and processes underlying craftwork are much the same regardless of the craft, and there seems to me no good reason why some crafts should be the province of women and others of men. The fact that the division of craft labour differs between cultures suggests that social expectations and traditions are more important than any 'natural' difference in ability between the sexes. In other countries, for example, women do thatch – although they may well be assigned to make the temporary roofs while the men make the permanent ones, or to produce the woven straw covering while the men produce the roof structure, or to repair the roofs that the men have made. In this country, thatching has always been a traditionally male activity. I'd like that to change.

PART THREE

MAKING IT WORK

CRAFT ON THE MARKET

Angharad Thomas

CRAFT FAIRS
The sale trauma

Angharad Thomas was educated as a geographer,
but knitting has captured her heart and mind. Despite
the emotional traumas of selling that she describes,
to her it is preferable to working as a secondary school
teacher.

You must have been to a craft fair, either as a craftswoman or as a potential customer. Craft fairs can be all things to all
people: a chance to become rich and famous; a chance to see lots of ideas
to try out at home; an afternoon out; the lucky break; somewhere to take
the usually unwilling children.

It starts for the craftworker weeks, perhaps months, before. The plain
brown envelope comes through the letterbox – no, it's not a grant from
the Crafts Council for £1,000, but an invitation to participate in a craft fair:

> The committee for the rebuilding of Exborough Parish Church
> are holding a Grand Craft Fair on Saturday 11th December and
> are inviting craftsmen [sic] to participate. A table will cost £10
> for the day, a half-table will cost £6.50 for the day, 10 per
> cent of your profit will go to the church mice

and so on. The tear-off slip is completed and posted first class (in case all
the tables go before your tear-off slip is received by the organisers).

The date is marked in the diary and on the calendar and work begins.
A six feet by two and a half feet trestle table suddenly seems a vast
acreage to have to fill. But never mind, there's some stuff in a suitcase
upstairs that didn't go at the last one, so that's a start. And there are one
or two things the family are wearing that once washed and pressed
shouldn't look too bad. You can label them 'sold' and that always looks
encouraging.

What to make? Jumpers, cardigans, pullovers? No, none of those – you
will have to charge too much and at least half the customers will be
expecting the event to be no more than a glorified jumble sale. Hats,
scarves, leg-warmers – smaller things that people might be tempted to
buy as presents? That's it, you'll aim at a dozen or so scarves and hats,
plus some things for display only – then people may be tempted to order
something for themselves. Better have a sheet of blurb, perhaps with an

order form. That takes some while to write. You agonise over it, change it a hundred times, and then finally duplicate it. It is all time when you should be making things, but perhaps you can't get down to being creative anyway, and sorting out the bureaucracy is a good excuse to put it off.

The day creeps nearer – the pile of scarves gradually grows. So does the panic and you wish you had not wasted those earlier days on your bureaucracy. The evening before everything needs labels: 'Made by . . .'. You get sick of seeing your own name so many times and wonder if you're some kind of maniac. You shamelessly call yourself 'fool' in a loud voice as you find the suitcase that has the craft fair tack in it: a pair of cotton sheets dating from your teens when you'd seen some trendy film or magazine with black sheets. Never mind, just the thing for covering a rough church hall trestle table. The first craft fair you went to you didn't have anything to cover the table and the carefully crafted goods looked out of place collecting splinters.

Back to the suitcase. Black sheets. Drawing pins. Tacks. Small hammer. Pins. Safety pins. Business cards. Two hundred order forms – you'll end up using three. Trendy plastic gaily coloured coathangers for hanging things on. Paper bags. Order book.

Then another suitcase for the work. All folded so neatly, so carefully. Leave the lid up overnight. Packed lunch. Make a flask in the morning – better then.

Up early in the morning – fifteen miles to go and you want to be set up in good time. The hall is open from 9 am, so that gives you an hour to get sorted.

In the car park when you arrive it's all go. People are carrying in what look like whole shop counters. Again you curse the inadequacy of your display system – black sheet and brightly coloured coathangers. Never mind, lug it all in, where's the table? Good to get a spot near the entrance door – by the time the punters get across the room they've usually spent the quid they've budgeted.

It must be easier to undress in public than put on a display of craft work. Here's my heart, here's my soul, say the garments, looking very sad all of a sudden. Why don't *I* paint dogs' heads on black velvet, you ask yourself? That stall looks really good.

Get the table all set out, at least the colours are bright. Thank goodness you brought your friend's Christmas cards to sell for her, they fill the end of the table nicely.

The doors open at 10 am and there you are, behind your table, ensconced on a church hall chair, novel or knitting in hand, trying hard to look distanced. And failing dismally. The time passes even more slowly than when you're teaching a class of teenagers last thing on Friday afternoon. Funny, you hadn't thought that possible.

Eleven o'clock eventually arrives. By this time the place is quite full. The man on the table next to you has sold at least one stained and leaded

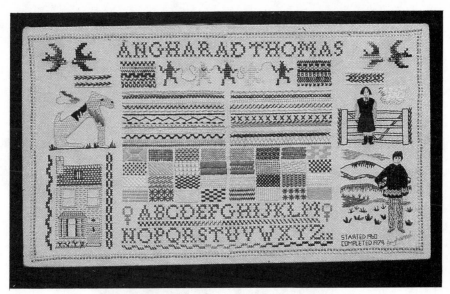

Embroidered sampler by Angharad Thomas

glass ashtray. In the worst possible taste, in your opinion. On the other side of you is a lady painter who gives you a friendly smile. She looks as if she will look after your stall while you vanish for a pee.

Two women stop by the table and start discussing *your* work loudly. Is it hand or machine? Oh, can't be hand, this is too even. I always think machine knitting isn't as nice as hand, don't you? What a price – you'd get one in a shop for half that, etc., etc.

The people who visit craft fairs seem to have little or no idea that the people sitting behind the tables have anything to do with the work on the tables in front of them. However, you attempt to hide behind your paperback – not easy – and they go away.

Someone comes up and buys a packet of Christmas cards. They give you a £5 note for 40p, so that's all your well organised float gone.

Then, suspense mounting, a woman starts examining the scarves. She's showing real interest – a woman of taste – tries one on, then another. Excitement mounts. Will she, won't she – yes she does; she'll have the blue one. Hooray! Only sell three more and the cost of the stall will be covered. Four more people and you've covered your petrol too. Still, that's being optimistic.

The day drags on. You eat your packed lunch, feeling like a bear eating buns at the zoo. The coffee in the flask is still hot so that's good – a cup now and leave one for later. The stained glass man has sold over £100 worth of the bad taste ashtrays and trinket boxes – he goes to a craft fair most weekends, he says, can't keep up with them. The lady painter seems to be doing as badly as you are.

ANGHARAD THOMAS

Acrylic and lurex 'Urban Jumper' by Angharad Thomas

write his name and address in your order book and put all the details down. Yes, it'll be ready in about three weeks.

That has made the day worthwhile; well, just about worthwhile. You sink behind the paperback and feel you can look the public in the eye again.

Four o'clock. It's thinning out now – only an hour to go. You discuss craft fair economics with the lady painter who has sold virtually nothing either. She says that the consensus is that very few people have had a successful day (the stained glass man is an obvious exception). Where she has picked up that consensus from you don't know and you don't ask – reassured in your collective failure.

A few more come and pick things around without buying. You tidy the table up after them, arranging things so artistically, how can they be resisted?

At ten to five you think, 'Blow it,' and start packing up. The stained glass man has hardly anything left to pack away. The potters start appearing with crates and newspaper. What a performance packing pottery is – one broken pot and that's your profit for the day gone.

That's the good thing about textiles – shove it all in the suitcases and

An interesting-looking person comes and talks about having a jumper made to order. Yes, you can do that style, yes, you can get those colours in pure wool. How much will it be – roughly? Yes, that'll be all right. You go home. Lug it all back in the house. Sort out the cases. They're too full for the end of the day – still, it'll all come in handy for Christmas presents.

That night your head swims with faces and noise. Must order the wool for that jumper. Yes, you covered your costs, but how! It's definitely the last craft fair you're going to – it's just not worth it.

Until the next plain brown envelope comes through the door – oh, that's a good area, lots of rich people live there, the table is only £5, it's worth a try.

Clare Rendell

THE WIDER LAST OF SHOEMAKING

Clare Rendell has spoken to many shoemakers
and found that, for all of them, 'large amounts of
money or success were not high priorities' and that the
interest of their businesses lay beyond the growth
and profit motive.

The revival of shoemaking as a craft began in the early
1970s. The success story of Rachel Floater and her American partner
Robert can provide a context for the methods and problems of women
shoemakers working now. Rachel started making ethnic sandals at a time
when demand was great and English suppliers were rare. From the
hand-to-mouth existence of selling in the Portobello Road market in West
London, her partnership expanded into a chain of London shops which
included the Yak, Plum and Natural Shoe Stores. She began to import
large quantities from America and Denmark and had less time left to make
her own. Keeping the books and working in an informal group turned
into the time-consuming big business tasks of administration and personnel
management. Rachel found that success had ruined what she found
enjoyable about craftwork, and she left the business when she found her
partner's ready response to the momentum of growth conflicted with her
own interest in the practical work of making sandals. Rachel's success,
ironically, rebounded against her, and her pioneering attempt to provide
an alternative to the uncomfortable refinements of mass-produced shoes
has been largely appropriated in the 1980s by factories reverting to simple
shapes. (The same trend can be seen in a shop like Habitat which sports
a handcrafted image alongside its high-tech one.)

Rachel came to understand the pitfalls of craftwork via the unusual
route of success. But in fact all the women I have spoken to link their
work with what they want from life, and large amounts of money or
success are not high priorities. The element of control is a recurrent
theme. It implies a creative dialogue between their chosen style and
their customers' needs which is completely different from the popular
adaptations of the shoe trade, and for this reason I have concentrated
more on those who take control of their craft, rather than on women doing
specialised work in factories or with established bespoke shoemakers.

The present decline in the industry has its roots at the beginning of the twentieth century, when less developed countries became increasingly able to produce shoes instead of exporting the cheap raw materials. The reaction to this decline in shoemaking can take two forms. One is a game attempt to combat economic realities, and the best example is a group of skilled women closers (those who stitch uppers) in Fakenham who took over their factory when the owners wanted to shut it down.[1] The firm had been a small outworkers' base for a bigger company, so the market for their goods disappeared with the change in management. Despite strong leadership and a grant, the women were forced to expand their market by making luggage and leather clothes, and the shoemaking side declined.

The other response is a positive dissatisfaction with the industry as it stands and an attempt to restore shoemaking as a craft without rejecting the machinery and practical insights that industrial development has brought. This new definition of the craft has an impact on the traditional commercial approach as well as on our ideas about fashion. Any woman who aims to earn her living by making shoes must compete with mass production, with fashion as its most powerful tool. One of the central principles of traditional economics is that growth lowers unit costs. Industry can produce shoes more cheaply than craftswomen and can ensure a steady demand by means of constantly changing fashion. Even women opposed to commercial fashion may prefer to buy trainers or sandals from less developed countries. Faced with this limited market for their shoes, the biggest problem for craftswomen is to keep their prices down while resisting the goal of traditional commerce which would mean growth of their business out of their hands and its consequent reversion from craft to industry.

Women's experience of learning the craft and turning it into a business can depart in many different ways from the traditional commercial approach. At a Welsh co-operative of women shoemakers, Marged Shoes, one woman was formally trained and the others learnt from her.[2] The Devonian Green Shoes women learnt the essentials from a local business and then developed through practice and mutual support. Two of the women I met – Barbara Holmes, who learnt the craft from friends, and Dolores, a former student at Cordwainers College in Hackney, London – are keener to work alone, more for practical reasons such as insufficient machinery than from a reluctance to share their skills.

Making shoes may be divided into three separate activities: making lasts, uppers and soles. Few shoemakers make their own lasts, preferring supple leather combined with flat soles which mould to the shape of the foot, and seeing the use of lasts as a way to develop their skills in the future. Leather is still the preferred material for uppers. Despite a growing concern for animal rights, materials like plastic and fabric are only used by a minority, because they are not so durable, nor so economically viable as leather. Making uppers remains a creative activity even in the industrial sector, and formal shoemaking courses tend to concentrate on design. Luna Hawxwell at Marged Shoes found this neglect of the production process in favour of design an isolating experience when she studied at Cordwainers College. But it would also be true to say that Cordwainers is among the colleges beginning to pay greater attention to the craft, and Dolores makes the point that students are encouraged to learn about small businesses.

Whatever the emphasis of particular courses, they can be a useful starting point from which to teach other women informally. The alternative to a course is apprenticeship to a shoemaker, and this is the direction that Thea Cadabra took. She learnt the essentials from a Turkish shoemaker in about five months and then proceeded by trial and error with her own ideas. The strength of individual ideas is a noticeable characteristic of women shoemakers. In the case of Nancy McCarthy, who makes shoes on her own, it was the failure to find shoes she liked that made her persuade two friends to teach her their skills. Sue, who lives and works

in North London, studied at more than one college and, after training, decided to concentrate on shoes for girls since they were less well catered for than women. Green Shoes were determined to challenge industrial invasion of the craft and they work entirely by hand. Women who learn shoemaking through less formal channels than courses or apprenticeships tend to be more committed to a collective approach; the Green Shoes women, disillusioned after their mixed shoemaking co-operative collapsed, have found that the process of teaching just other women brings closer links and makes their shoemaking a way of life.

These different approaches to training are accompanied by different priorities in making a living from the craft. Barbara Holmes began with machinery and materials passed on by others, and is happy with a small business as long as she can support herself by it. Thea Cadabra, too, wants to preserve enjoyment as the main motive of her work. Sue's responsibilities as a single parent impose their own priorities on her lifestyle. Her concentration on girls' shoes also demanded a far greater initial outlay on lasts; taking account of half-sizes and different widths from

Shoe designs by Green Shoes, drawn by Pamela Innes

ages five to fifteen, she calculated she would need seventy-two different pairs.

With collectives the issues are more complex. Growth is built into their approach to shoemaking in the desire to share their skills, and groups tend to expand and contract in unpredictable ways. The initial outlay on a workshop and tools can also be greater. But the experimental flexibility of co-operatives does not endear such enterprises to bodies who might provide loans or grants. Marged Shoes found that their applications were not taken seriously unless they required a large sum and had already received a grant from another source. They were advised to increase their prices to help cover their costs, but resisted this as a short-sighted solution which would restrict rather than expand their market. Money was finally raised through small interest-free loans from other women. Green Shoes found a business studies evening class useful, but Marged suggests that the self-help principle worked more efficiently, other co-operatives having a better idea than official channels of advice about the sort of problems that arise. It is certainly ironic that women who try to build up a business from scratch based on modest assessments of their financial needs are obliged to talk in traditional commercial terms of big money if they want to receive any help at all.

Whatever the size of the business, assuming a living is to be earned from it, the main task is stabilising its growth through initial lack of interest and subsequent seasonal variations. Marged Shoes work largely through mail order, and they cope with seasonal variations by adjusting the pattern of advertising. Other women rely more on personal appearances at markets and fairs. Nancy McCarthy had little success at a London stall, so she moved to Wales to improve her skills and has found a better response at the markets there.[3] The method of selling through markets and mail order is very different from traditional retail outlets. Most people still go to shops to buy shoes, and the shift to these other methods will only be gradual, as benefits like better fit and greater choice in design and colour are recognised. Green Shoes enjoys the personal relationship built up with customers, most of whom come in to be measured and choose a design, and see this link as a necessary though time-consuming part of the business.

The shoemakers I spoke to designed mainly, though not exclusively, for women, and their work is determined by their ideas about female identity. Barbara Holmes, for instance, likes the fact that her flat shoes give women maximum comfort and the ability to run if necessary. Many women are concerned to preserve the health of their feet. The need for manufacturers to adapt new designs cheaply can result, for example, in badly designed pointed toes and lack of support at the instep.[4] Sue sees the battle between style and comfort as especially dangerous to girls, when the pressures to conform to fashionable models are greatest and damage to feet is most likely. Concern for health was strong in the hippy era, and it was accompanied by a more intuitive approach to design, like wrapping patterns around the feet. David and Inger Rink explain this method in their book *Shoes for Free People*.[5]

At the other end of the spectrum, Thea Cadabra prizes sophistication and variety, pointing out that high heels can give assertiveness and theatricality to a woman. Heels are not innately submissive though the shadow of vulnerability behind the aggressively pointed heel is a favourite male fantasy. The artist Alexis Hunter has shown that the idea of the shoe as bondage is still a potent symbol. In her photographic sequences 'Approach to Fear' of 1977, an uncomfortable-looking shoe is removed, toyed with, and finally burned.[6] The foot itself has an elaborate history of erotic associations closely linked with power relationships between men and women. Arched feet are thought to imply good breeding and an active libido. The writer W. A. Rossi offers proof that attempts to secure dainty feet by footbinding were not confined to China.[7] The same taste for deformation is behind the traditional male preference for women in high heels which can change the posture and appearance of the body as well as the way of walking.

Experiment and change are the crucial factors in this discussion of shoes; inevitably so, since people have always modified nature by resorting to the artificial, and the recognition of contrasts is central to the way the brain works. Such constant and compulsive reappraisal finds an ideal partner in fashion. Susceptibility to fashion exists in all societies: it springs from each individual's self-image and takes the form of imitating (or not imitating) something different. Unless they are hermits, people can't avoid making statements by what they wear, so fashion extends to imitation among all groups, not simply those vulnerable to commercial pressures. Fashion certainly has an important commercial role in encouraging people to buy new shoes instead of being content with one durable and comfortable pair. This is why anticipating fashion was an important part of Dolores' course at Cordwainers.

It is necessary to establish what fashion is and the way it operates if the challenge of women shoemakers is to be fully appreciated. Conventional fashions are produced by the division of the industrial labour system, where the creative and manufacturing elements are separated. Commercial shoes tend to reflect this system because they are designed as accessories to a wider current look in clothes and behaviour. The creative process in industry is thus very different from the craft ideal of one person working through each stage of shoe production and experimenting along the way. The approach to customers is also very different. Mass production and consumption have developed patterns in which conformity is the dominant theme and the sense of identity rests on how one appears to others. Fashion is also seen as more important to women – a convenient confirmation of her role as arbiter of appearances in home and family, which perpetuates our type of society.

All the women shoemakers I spoke to challenge conventional fashion.

'La Bonne' shoes by Thea Cadabra

Marged and Green Shoes prize eternal features like comfort and durability, and the individuality of their shoes arises from the fact that they are made to measure in chosen combinations of colour and design. Barbara concentrates on simple comfortable shapes which she decorates in paint or appliqué. Thea Cadabra's challenge is bolder. She starts from her own enjoyment of materials and sense of humour, hoping to spark the imagination of others with elaborate shoes on themes including a storm, a vampire, a dragon, a broken egg and a bumper car. Her recent work is more sophisticated, and a shoe like 'La Bonne' (the maid), with its frilly apron trim and legs on tip toe for heels, makes fun of the revival of Nippy waitresses and romantic formality in dress. Any concern for conformity, for how the wearer appears to others, would be crushed by these witty reflections on life.

As Thea Cadabra says, the only way to learn about shoemaking is to do it.[8] This feeling that the mystique has been taken out of the craft is the greatest contribution of modern women shoemakers. A fresh, practical approach also dominates their methods of business, and it is based on a realistic grasp of present economic conditions as well as a determination to enjoy their lives. The Green Shoes women comment on the exhilarating feeling of being self-employed and suggest that they are working largely from commonsense. Thea Cadabra's move to France was motivated as much by her resistance to commercial and city pressures as by the fact that her work was increasingly sold abroad. Even when they have been trained in the traditional commercial way, the women that I've spoken to protect their imaginations and develop new standards for reassessing their customers' needs. They have shown that the experience of shoemaking can be creative for many, and its greatest strength lies in the enthusiasm to pass on their skills – as in the Marged weekend workshops, where women can walk away after two days in a pair of shoes they have made, and sometimes designed, themselves.

Eira Benton at work in her cobbling shop

Eira Benton

COBBLING

Essentially, craftspersons do their work because it is
creatively satisfying to them. Eira Benton lives in
Wolverhampton. She is a retired cobbler and she
talked to Sue Scott about her enthusiasm for her
work.

I got interested in shoe repairing as a child by watching my uncle mend
the family's shoes. When I was a little older I visited other shoe repairers
to see how they did it. I used to sit in the cobblers' shops in Compton,
rolling their threads for them, and I picked up the craft in that way. I taught
myself really; you have to be gifted, then it's easy and enjoyable.

My husband was a cobbler when I met him. I worked in his shop but
he never really liked the work, so he turned the shop over to me and
went into nursing. At first customers didn't treat me seriously because
they couldn't believe that a woman could do the job properly. Later
though, when they knew more about me, if my husband answered the
shop bell, they would say, 'I want to see the lady please.' I felt very proud
of that.

I belonged to the Boot Traders' Association and you had to be a skilled
craftsman to be a member. I was the only woman there together with
forty men. We had meetings every month in Bilston to discuss the state
of the trade and the price of leather. It wasn't all business, though; we
used to go on outings to the tanneries – Warrington tannery, for example,
or Goodyears where they made the 'sticker' soles.

I always looked after my own tools. My finishing machine was powered
by a ½ h.p. motor and I had to take it to pieces regularly, oil it and empty
the dust bag. My husband didn't know how to do it and I even had to
dismantle it for the man who bought it when I sold the shop because he
didn't know anything about it either.

I never met other women who were interested in cobbling, though
they were amazed at my skills. Shoe repairing wasn't a well paid job but
I was given enough praise and appreciation to make it worth while. It used
to take me about half an hour to sole and heel a pair of man's boots.
During the war I used to mend the Dutch soldiers' boots from the Princess
Irene Brigade stationed at Perton. When the brigade left, trade was bad
and I looked after two doctors' surgeries to bring in some extra money.

I had to dust their desks, tidy up, and put out the cards for their patients. With that, and the shoe repairing, my housework and meals to cook for my husband and son, I was very busy. It was a long day. I had to get up early to see my husband off to work. He used to catch the 5.25 am bus to the hospital. Then at about 8 o'clock I'd trot round to the doctors' and start work there.

In the evening I used to enjoy going with my cousin to the Hippodrome in Wolverhampton. On one occasion a friend promised to get me a ticket to see Charlie Kunz the pianist, but the next day he said that Charlie wanted to see me instead. Charlie gave me the job of repairing his shoes. He had to have very thin soles so that he could touch the piano pedals very lightly. He used to send his shoes to me by post from Middlesex.

I traded under the name of 'True Walk' because I used to build up shoes on one side, or put irons on the boots of disabled people in order to correct their walk. I used to put my heart into every job. There was a man living in Claverley who had a peg leg and he was fed up because he only wore out one shoe from every pair that he bought. I took all the odd left shoes to pieces, soaked the leather because it was new and hadn't been worn, hammered it to fit the right last and then built it up. He was as pleased as punch.

I still get asked to mend the odd pair, but the trade has been ruined by cheap rubbish which can't be repaired. Customers used to say that my repairs lasted for ages. A man stopped me the other day as I was getting on to the bus. I used to repair his shoes before I retired eleven years ago and he was wearing a pair which I had repaired then and they were still going strong.

One thing which I enjoyed was reading people's characters from the way they walked. I didn't let them hear though, because in some cases it might have offended them. A small hole in the middle of the sole means that the wearer has good sense. A broader shallow hole means an easy-going nature. If the shoe shows signs of wear on the inside, halfway between the toe and the waist, it means the wearer is conceited, whereas if the shoe is worn down on the outside, it means reliability.

I don't need to visit the chiropodist. People ask me how, at seventy-two years of age, I've gone through life without corns or bunions. I always say, 'Proper shoes, wide enough, that don't pinch. If you look after your shoes, your feet will look after themselves.'

Sara Bowman

HIDDEN WORLDS
Homeworking on the machine

For women who work as highly skilled machinists at home, generally in order to supplement an inadequate family income, the freedom to 'choose' craftwork is an illusion. Work at home is the only alternative to the factory with child-minder. Sara Bowman describes the exploitation which highlights divisions of race and class, as well as gender.

In the hidden world of the homeworkers, skilled machinists and finishers undertake the same work as factory workers, often with additional tasks and responsibilities, but in the confines of their own homes. Ever since the Industrial Revolution, the fashion and textile industry has relied heavily on these women to make up and decorate dresses, more so since the advent of mass-produced clothing.

London is the centre of the British fashion trade and supports a thriving homeworker industry, with most work subcontracted to small manufacturing units to reduce costs. These units, with less than twenty employees, then farm out contract work to individual homeworkers, who are mostly mothers of young children. Work is seasonal, and during peak periods, it is needed very quickly. The homeworking workforce is 'Flexible, cheap, vulnerable and unorganised'.[1] The majority of employers regard homeworkers as self-employed, so they receive little or none of the legal protection afforded to other workers. 'The Homeworkers Protection Bill, which would give homeworkers employees' rights and status, has been introduced twice to the House of Commons in recent years and has been defeated on both occasions.'[2]

These women have always been denied any acknowledgement of their craft skills or traditions, and are low paid. As the present economic situation worsens, women are being forced to work up to seventy hours a week for £30. This works out at 43p an hour. Out of this they have to pay for electricity, their heating, insurance, machine hire and machine maintenance. The average statutory hourly wage for a factory machinist is £1.45, though few are paid this; most of the work is piece work and earnings depend on skill, speed and the hours one puts in.[3]

Through contacts and chance encounters I was able to meet women, mostly second-generation immigrants (Greek and Turkish Cypriots, and West Indians), who introduced me to their family homeworking network. Many of the older women don't speak English, but their daughters, brought up with different expectations, are very articulate about the plight of their mothers. They themselves avoid homework where they can and aim for managerial positions. Today the majority of homeworkers are the newest immigrants, Asians from Pakistan and Bangladesh. In general their families are actively involved in the organisation of the small manufacturing units. Cultural barriers, language problems from the outset, together with the invisibility of homeworking women, mean that it is very difficult indeed to penetrate these private and hidden worlds. In addition to cultural barriers, women are reluctant to discuss their work for fear of alerting tax officials or social security officers. Physical isolation, together with the difficulties of communication, contribute to their oppression.

CADENCE

Memorial Road, East Ham, runs adjacent to a busy railway line. The rows of nineteenth-century workers' houses are painted green; some have small gardens. It is here in London's East End, in houses like these or in council flats, that women sit for hours, behind their lace curtains and in front of their industrial sewing machines (often padded to conceal the noise), making up dresses for the rag trade. Cadence Martin lives here. She was born in Jamaica and came to England after she was married at twenty-two. She has worked in the British fashion industry for over twenty-five years. Cadence first worked in a factory and started at home, like so many other women, in order to cope with the demands of her young family and as an alternative to a full-time job. Despite working longer hours at home with the additional tasks of delivery, packing, unpacking and collecting work, sorting out fabric pieces, providing and maintaining her own equipment and paying for the electricity, she still earned less money than she had in the factory. Consequently, as soon as her children were old enough to attend school she went back to the factory, but continued homework in the evenings to supplement her income.

'When my first children were young I did shift work during the day and my husband was able to look after the children because he worked nights. After my fourth child was born, I decided to work from home. I bought a second-hand sewing machine for £58, that was in 1965, they now cost anything from £250. I continued working for the same firm, doing the same work. I started at six in the morning, and after getting the children off to school, I worked till they came home again, and then often till two o'clock the following morning.

'I was alone at home, with the baby, working in a corner of my bedroom every day. But when you have children, you have to cope somehow, even when it means working round the clock to finish an order; there's no one to stand up for you, you either take it or leave it. I taught two Ghanaian women how to machine, how to sew the seams straight, and put the parts together, so that they could get a job. One of them brought me a lovely cup and saucer by way of thanking me when she did get a job. It was the first time anyone had done something like that for me – and I still have the cup and saucer, I treasure them.

'Nobody cares about you when you are working from home; you have to hide away. Sometimes I took in children as well, to make ends meet. Machining is a highly skilled job, but no one recognises us – we do the work, the firm gets the praise; we don't get a chance to show our talents.

'In 1978 I went home to Jamaica, and on my return started work in a fur factory doing linings. I worked from eight till three, then I collected my son from school and brought him back to the factory with me, and worked through till six, and still took work home with me. The boss in the factory was a good man and I felt relaxed. I've worked in some places where the governor was very mean, so we did things to the machines or wasted cotton so he would have to buy more; it was our way of getting back at him. I then started machining the fur coats at home, I can do three a night. Each coat has seventy-five pelts which have to be sewn together, and for each coat we are paid £2.75, but out of that has to come 50p a night for electricity, whereas in the factory we were paid £2.80 and they paid the electricity. The coats sold in Harrods for £700. My boss wasn't that good, he wouldn't sell me one at cost.'

Two years ago a friend of Cadence who worked as a fashion technician in the local Polytechnic told her of a School of Independent Studies which ran there. It welcomed mature students from diverse backgrounds and experience, and accepted Cadence to study textile print[4]. She eventually hopes to set up her own business, to be run as a co-operative.

SARA BOWMAN

'Today as a student I am very happy; it's a great relief not to be machining at home, all the time killing yourself just to keep the job. Learning to print has altered my life – I am happy with it. When I first started the course I knew nothing about printing; I came on the course to do pattern cutting, but seeing the print room gave me ideas, and talking to tutors helped. Because I can't draw, I tear paper to form things I want, or I use a paint brush. I really enjoy hand-painting and when I saw the Raoul Dufy exhibition, I realised he was using the same kind of brush strokes as I do, that was exciting. Many of my designs are of West Indian scenes.

'I think everyone should have a chance to learn new skills; there are many people out there who can do as well as me or better – we underestimate ourselves. When we get the chance, which is sometimes hard, people begin to realise that we are not all duffy, that we can do many things. The beauty about it is seeing the things you have done that you never believed you could do.'

LINDA
Linda lives in Finsbury Park, at the heart of the Greek Cypriot community in North London. It is a thriving fashion manufacturing area; the streets are filled with small factories and specialist trade suppliers operating behind shop and showroom façades. For over twenty years Linda's relatives have worked in the clothing industry.

'First I trained as an office worker, then after I married and had a child, I decided to learn machining because machinists earned good money. My mother is Greek Cypriot – she worked in a dress factory at the time and the manager agreed to take me on there, provided she trained me. After a few years we both left the factory and started machining from home. In the early sixties there wasn't so much outwork, but by the early seventies, when Greek and Turkish Cypriots began to open dress factories around here, homeworking opportunities expanded. To immigrant women who don't speak the language, and who need to work and earn money, machining at home is ideal. Even today, after twenty years, some of our relatives don't speak English. It suits our culture where women, especially unmarried ones, are very protected; working from home, you can't get into trouble.

'I found jobs through the local paper. I always worked for Cypriot firms, and dealt directly with the factory. It's all piece work, the wages depend on the speed and the hours you put in. I'm a good machinist and I work fast. When you're experienced you can earn good money, but those who are self-taught earn much less. Making up cheap clothes is a strain; working with better quality clothes is more satisfying, and it pays more. Machining is skilled work; as soon as a style changes (which happens regularly) you have to spend a day working out the quickest way to make the garment – there can be as many as fifteen different pieces in a dress, and you have to work out how to put them together. I worked from nine o'clock till six, and sometimes at weekends. My husband didn't like the noise of the industrial machine; he wanted to relax after his work, so I did try not to use it while he was at home. You have to force yourself to sit at that machine, it's hard work and very lonely; you don't do it if you have a choice, but many women don't have that.'

THELMA
Thelma White was born in England, but her parents are Jamaican. She lives on the outskirts of London on an old, dark, brick housing estate, with her husband and four daughters. Her mother was a machinist who worked at home on piece work, but Thelma was brought up to have different expectations. However, despite her training in credit control, it was the cost of childcare together with the difficulties of finding work with flexible hours which could accommodate the needs of her children that forced her into machining at home.

'It was after my third daughter was born that I began working at home. I couldn't afford the cost of childcare, it was £18 a week for each of them to be looked after by a registered child-minder, added to which I had to supply milk, food and nappies.

'Very few firms provide machines; you have to supply your own. I bought mine on hire purchase, and I'm still paying for it. My first job was sewing blouses for 30p each; now the rate varies between 60p and 70p for dresses. The lower the price, the more particular they seem about the work; but you can't be too fussy, you take what you can get. Whatever you earn each week is a help. If you work it out – the time, the cost of the machine, the loss of sleep – it's crazy, but you don't notice that you're running at a loss. All you know is that what you have earned is a help now. Without it you couldn't survive, you're up against the wall and don't feel there's another choice. If I worked in a factory I would earn more, but the long hours – eight till six – and the cost of looking after the children make that impossible. People, society, should do something for women like me who have children and need to work.'

Thelma has managed to do something for herself, and maybe for a few other women like her. A year ago an anonymous neighbour reported Thelma to her local council for illegally running a business from home (homeworking is outlawed in most council properties, although some councils have amended tenancy agreements to make it possible, and others are trying to). Her need to continue to earn an income prompted her to set up her own homeworking unit. She took it upon herself to obtain work from local factories and was able to find suitable machinists through advertisements in local papers. Like other women, Thelma took the classic way out of homeworking, yet she saw that it did not represent a real alternative: 'I saw my own way out of machining by supplying others with work, but I wanted to help those people too.'

Thelma wanted a unit where women could work flexible hours to fit

*Three faces of
homeworking*

in with schools and where a crèche could be provided for those with pre-school children. The Greater London Enterprise Board gave her the opportunity to set up such a unit locally, and with grant aid the unit ran as a co-operative. Opportunities like these must be encouraged and supported.

WHAT IS TO BE DONE?

The Trades Board Acts of 1909 and 1918 were the result of three decades of active public outcry and campaigning against the appalling conditions of the homeworker. They established a minimum wage for both piece work and factory work. Despite legislation, minimum wages were not adhered to, and the situation continued as before, away from public notice. It was not until the 1970s that pressure group organisations once again sought to make the homeworking issue public and visible. Throughout the United Kingdom, a large variety of projects have been developed as a response to the needs of homeworkers; they reflect the character and needs of specific areas. Local projects aim to make the issue of homeworking visible, to bring homeworkers out of their isolation, to provide opportunities for them to meet for support, to give advice on conditions of work, health, safety and tax, and to provide opportunities for homeworkers to acquire independence through retraining.

The Low Pay Unit was set up in 1974 as a national independent research and campaign organisation to highlight and change the conditions of the low paid. It has acted as a pressure group for legal change and at grass-roots level through the West Midland Low Pay Unit.

In 1982 the London Boroughs Association set up a working group in an attempt to clarify the position of the homeworker. It recommended that the London boroughs adopt a positive policy and strategy to deal with homeworking issues. The Greater London Council was an important funding body until 1986. It adopted a three-point policy and commitment on homeworking, which included policing and monitoring the contract agreements with firms which supplied goods to their departmental offices. Secondly, by setting up an economic infrastructure of co-operative development agencies, it helped provide initiatives and alternatives to homeworking. Thirdly, it provided funds to support local homeworking projects on a grass-roots basis in the London boroughs. The GLC is now dead, but in some cases the local boroughs have taken over its initiatives.

One such project is based in Greenwich, and was developed as a response to the needs of the community; it was set up by a women's collective based at Plumstead Community Centre in 1978. From its inception it has worked closely with homeworkers in the borough. Staffed by a collective of four, it is multi-racial, and includes a Punjabi-speaking worker, who is in close contact with Asian women in the borough. The project offers advice surgeries, skill and assertiveness training courses (funded by the Industrial Common Ownership Movement), and advice on alternative ways of working, such as co-operatives. The project campaigns on issues such as health and safety and, when time allows, workers give outside talks and discussions.

KATHY

Kathy is a highly skilled machinist who was a homeworker for several years after her child was born, before she took a job in a polytechnic fashion department as a fashion technician. She still continued homework to supplement her income. She felt frustrated by the confines of her job, and wanted to set up her own business, although she didn't know how to. But she did know that she had skill and talent: 'I know it sounds stupid, but at the end of my fingers, I have all this capability – it's an invisible drive – I find my work easy. Sometimes it can be a challenge; if something is difficult I try to master it.'

A talk given by Mary Sahni of the Greenwich Homeworker Project to fashion students at the polytechnic was the initiative that Kathy needed to change her situation. For the first time she heard her experience articulated. After informal discussions with the project about setting up a co-op with some other women, she decided to increase her skills and requested a day release programme from her employers to study pattern cutting as a first step to establishing a business venture.

Campaigns organised by local homeworking projects on issues such as health can provide a vital link in bringing homeworkers together, thus increasing their awareness of their situation, and can provide information on how to change it. The Greenwich Homeworker Project recently organised a highly successful campaign on the health hazards of glue. Utilising the press and local media, they encouraged homeworkers working with glue to contact them. For many of these women it was the first time that they had made contact with a group which gave not only practical advice, but support; it increased their awareness of the homeworking situation, and in some instances was a positive step forward to change and independence.

PAT

Pat, a homeworker, responded to the glue campaign; she describes how it affected her life and work.

'I first rang Mary in January 1984 after reading her advertisement in the *Mercury* newspaper about homeworking and the effects of glue. I had a long conversation with her, then brought the glue over for analysis. A few weeks later I came back to find out the results and had another long chat with them all, and then came to their open day with a friend. I found out there was life after housework and kids, but the glue was paramount in my mind. It made me angry that I was putting myself and my family at risk, and I realised that I wanted to do something about this issue since I personally knew about the work and the effects of the glue. I was and still am very angry that I was exploited and that others are being exploited. Mary was doing a campaign about glue and solvents and their potential dangers. I designed the poster for the campaign and was very pleased with the results. Because I am not very artistically minded and have never done anything like that before it gave me great satisfaction.

'I have also spoken to many women on homeworking and racism. I have learnt more in the two months I have been helping here than I have in the last eleven years of being a wife and mother. It has inspired me to look at my boring humdrum life and to improve my knowledge, to give what I have to offer, and to take what people of different backgrounds and cultures have to offer me. Without the help of the GHP I would still be staying at home, taking my Valium and feeling very sorry for myself. At least here I have found a challenge in my life; at last I feel that I have some personal satisfaction.'[5]

During the last few years, initiatives have been taken by social workers and community workers in setting up women's groups in areas with large ethnic populations. These have provided valuable support networks for homeworkers. Ostensibly these groups were set up to provide opportunities for isolated Asian women who, due to cultural constraints, were confined to their homes. They come together once or twice a week to meet, to share experiences and to learn new skills. The group provides a framework for new ideas and initiatives.

The Hounslow Asian Women's Group (HAWCC) was set up by social and community workers as a response to the needs of local Asian women, many of whom are isolated homeworkers. It has been running since 1982 and initially received grant aid from the GLC. Seventy-five women come together each week to the Millan group (which, literally translated, means meeting for pleasure), for discussion and skill sessions. They have a comprehensive programme of activities, including English classes, video training sessions, keep fit, cooking and sewing classes. For many women, it's often the only contact they have with each other in a week. Within the group, initiatives have been taken to set up co-ops. Great care is taken to ease people into business projects, for although the co-op way of working is intrinsic to Asian culture and women are used to working within the extended family unit, for a co-op to be commercially successful involves a degree of confidence and skill which is often lacking in new co-op ventures generally, reducing them to short term businesses. A Hounslow consumer group has also developed from within the HAWCC Millan group. This enables women to buy food collectively from a warehouse at wholesale prices.

HAWCC provides a support network for homeworkers within the group. Several women found the confidence and initiative to bargain successfully for higher piece work rates. Upskilling sewing sessions, run twice a week, mean that the women are able to expand their skills, enabling them ultimately to acquire a greater degree of independence.

They learn to make shalwar-kamez, the traditional Punjabi suits which are their everyday dress; they are costly to buy. Shalwar-kamez are now being produced commercially by women.

The success of HAWCC has meant that similar initiatives have taken place in neighbouring boroughs. An Asian women's group has recently been established in the London borough of Hillingdon, which supports one of the largest Asian communities centred in Southall. Currently thirty-five Bengali homeworking women have been meeting twice a week for skill sessions. Many are homeworkers who either sew lace on to cami-knickers, earning six pence an hour, or construct Christmas crackers for 20 pence an hour. As the group receives no financial support (save for a £350 grant from the police) and has to cover minimum rent, it charges 25p a week to attend skill sessions in English and sewing; crèche facilities are available. For many women the cost is prohibitive. The long term plan is to create an industrial training centre to teach sewing and to improve women's skills so they can work collectively, making Punjabi suits.

The pressures and constraints of the commercial fashion world, which demand a flexible, cheap labour force where homeworkers are relegated to the basic machining and construction of clothes, have meant that the wealth of traditional craft skills which immigrant women have inherited are being eroded. In Tower Hamlets in East London, the Tower Hamlets Training Forum recognises this factor and has introduced pilot craft projects. Based in the Brick Lane area, a centre for small clothing manufacturing sweatshops and a thriving homeworking industry run by the Pakistani and Bengali communities, the Tower Hamlets Training Forum has introduced upskilling courses. Bengali homeworkers, contacted by outreach workers, participate. A new pilot project has recently been introduced to encourage immigrants to re-acquaint themselves with traditional craft skills such as embroidery, weaving and ceramics. Participants are being paid a living wage. It is anticipated that after training, half-way houses providing workshop and crèche facilities will be available, and newly skilled craftspeople will be linked to designers.

In London, workers from the various homeworking projects meet at the National Homeworking Group, to share richness of experience and provide a perspective on homeworking. Recently they have worked together to produce a fact pack for homeworkers, containing advice on homeworkers' rights, and information on health, safety, tax, social security and so on. The packs are distributed through voluntary organisations and local groups and projects. They have been translated into eleven different languages. The group played an instrumental part in the third National Homeworking Conference with its eight-point charter aiming to make homeworking visible and improve its conditions. Provided grant funding is forthcoming, initial homeworking projects will continue to provide important grassroots initiatives for change, enabling homeworkers to acquire greater independence through the acquisition of skills, and the opportunities to work collectively.

Today, homeworking is on the increase, and is a growth area in new technology industries. With the rise in multinational companies, homeworking has become an international phenomenon: a cheap, flexible, unorganised workforce is ideally suited to industry. Although pressure groups and networks have been established to change the conditions of the homeworker, the most important networks will be ones that come from the homeworkers themselves. It is crucial that both indoor workers and homeworkers expand our awareness and form networks which are international in scope and able to cross many social boundaries.

Sally Baxendale

ALL RIGHT ON THE NIGHT
Theatrical outworkers

Sally Baxendale describes a different kind of homeworking – for the theatre. Not low paid as machinists, and often from a more privileged class and race, theatre craftswomen are freelance workers who can share in the corporate effort, and the prestige, of each production.

You might be surprised to know that hats for the film 'Victor Victoria' (which won an Oscar for its costume design) were made in an attic in Sheffield; and that jewellery for the prestigious Granada Television production of 'King Lear' was created on a kitchen table in an equally unlikely place. All over this country, costumes, props, wigs and headdresses are being made by theatrical outworkers, and are seen on film and television screens the world over, as well as in our local and West End theatres. Much has been written about the technical and aesthetic aspects of the theatre as well as the performing side, but little observation has been made on theatrical craftspeople, their range of skills or their working conditions. This is an expanding industry employing many people and offering large numbers of skilled women a home-based, freelance career which, though not often lucrative, can provide a realistic living. I want to describe something of the working conditions of these freelance craftspeople – the costumiers, milliners, wig-makers, prop-makers and jewellers.

There are basically two kinds of freelance outworkers. First, there are those whose skills are so specialised that they couldn't be employed full-time in one company without doing other prop jobs as well. This group includes mask-makers and armourers, and a certain number of costumiers, usually men, who specialise, for instance, in men or women principals in opera, or in a particular period of costume. These men and women are at the top of the costume trade. Secondly, there are many costumiers and prop-makers for whom the autonomy and itinerancy of freelance work is more appealing than company employment. Amongst these are a great many women who can combine their work with domestic commitments. The industry, with its uneven demands, relies heavily on all these workers.

The main centres of employment are the theatres themselves, firms of costumiers serving the film industry, television, West End shows, opera and ballet companies. Most outworkers, many of whom have had a college training in fashion, theatre or fine arts, will have spent some years working 'in house' for one or more companies, learning their craft, gaining experience of the different branches of the entertainment industry and building contacts, before starting out on their own.

This is an ad hoc affair, operating largely on personal recommendation. The theatre and television network, though sprawling and nationwide, is closed, familial and protective. It is possible for the individual to know, or know of, most of her colleagues, and have an enormous acquaintance. Although there is the inevitable gossip and competitiveness, the grapevine is effective in disseminating information on outworkers and their skills. If somebody has the reputation of being only a so-so milliner, it won't be long before the word gets round that she's now resurfaced as an excellent mask-maker. It regularly happens that a woman never really leaves the company where she once had a full-time job (that is, when she has a baby or takes a less demanding job; people do get sick of the long hours in theatres, and sometimes try, usually unsuccessfully, to give it up). Although she will have been replaced, she is likely to be called on regularly as an outworker for large productions. A colleague from that company moving to another will take the new outworker's reputation for, say, expertise in men's period tailoring, to the new company. In this way, a circle of new clients is built up and a new career as a specialist formed.

This is an introverted industry; cosy and self-contained, but dominated by the urgency to get the show on. It can be a disorienting and isolating profession for outworkers. The transience of each production, and the often intense working relationships, the hard work and tension that build up towards opening night and the anti-climax after, can be physically and emotionally draining, leaving little energy for organising together. Sharing work facilities, comparing rates of pay, collating information on different companies, forthcoming productions or suppliers is informal and unsystematic. The National Association of Theatrical, Television and Kine Employees (NATKE) cannot adequately represent the interests of outworkers, although it has been effective in improving rates of pay and conditions for company employees, such as lighting and stage technicians. The annual subscription for a freelance, on a sliding scale, is one of the highest – unrealistic for many women who can only work part-time and sporadically. It also requires nomination from two members, which can be difficult to obtain when one is not in regular contact with one company, as can be access to a union representative. The Association of Cinematograph, Television and Allied Technicians (ACTT) operates a closed shop, and those wishing to work on films as costume supervisors and wardrobe

JOHN BAXENDALE

Sally Baxendale, freelance theatrical milliner

assistants go through the same procedures to get their ticket as other film technicians. However, many outworkers make for films by being subcontracted through costume hire firms. The Association of British Theatre Technicians (ABTT) is a non-union organisation, active in areas such as providing codes of practice for technicians, testing new materials for safety, providing technical advice to theatres, setting up trade shows of theatrical equipment and services, and training. They run many courses, full-time and day release, for electricians, sound engineers and stage technicians, and occasionally one- or two-day courses in a craft such as mask-making or a certain period in costume-cutting. Although they serve technicians well – with regular meetings, London and regional, a journal, and a London office with bar and library facilities – there is still a need for an effective national forum for theatrical outworkers. Women in Entertainment has launched a monthly newsletter which is of interest to non-performing women, and they are also compiling a register of theatre craftswomen.

The hourly rate for theatrical outworkers is more realistic than for many other home-based industries, probably between £5 and £15 per hour, depending on the expertise of the maker and the esotericism of the product. However, the sporadic and seasonal nature of the work demands careful budgeting. The customary advance payments on big jobs can help avert cash-flow problems, although credit for the bulk buying of basic materials like adhesives and haberdashery can be hard to come by. In its rates of pay this work is obviously much better than the traditional 'sweated' industries, but it does share some of their conditions. The hours can be punishing because of the deadline or changes in direction or design. Domestic circumstances, with masks drying in the airing cupboard, panfuls of dyeing feathers cooking next to the dinner, rolls of braid and boxes of sequins everywhere, can be as squalid as any nineteenth-century matchbox makers'. It may be impossible to estimate how many people work like this because of the frequent and easy mobility between company employment and outwork. My impression is that few women leave the business. I know several women, myself included, who worked to within days of the birth of their children and resumed shortly afterwards. Theatrical outwork does attract independent and individualistic women, like many of their sisters on the stage or in the other arts. These women are devoted to their work, the theatre and their large scattered acquaintance, and they thrive on the long hours and itinerancy.

This work differs structurally from cottage industries such as pottery, handloom weaving and patchwork, or fine arts such as photography, painting, printmaking and sculpture. It isn't entrepreneurial since a market doesn't have to be sought, and little capital is required as materials are mainly supplied and, of course, it differs in its lesser artistic autonomy. However, theatrical work does share with the more successful art or craft enterprises a speed and professionalism necessitated by the short production period. This is usually a matter of weeks, since measurements and fittings can't be had till the company is assembled and rehearsing. There is a firm deadline – hopefully the first dress rehearsal, but in extremis the opening night. And there is the need for a strong, durable product, since costumes and props take a hammering from energetic productions, long runs and location work, and must last decades in opera and repertoire, in which they are constantly revamped.

Central to the maker's career is the designer. Not only does the maker usually work to his or her specifications, but she relies on a good working relationship for getting more work and, through recommendations, work with other designers. Most designers will have a stable of their favourite makers with whom they feel they have a rapport. Having artistic rapport with a designer means being able to interpret and realise the designs, closing the gap between what is envisaged and what is put down on paper. The successful maker who is always in demand for prestigious productions is therefore not only technically competent but artistically empathetic as well, and is respected by designers as an equal. In any case, the relationship between the designer and maker is usually co-operative and consultative, the designer eliciting work from the maker's experience and expertise which fulfils his or her 'vision' for a production, rather as the director does with the actors. Many designers like to be actively involved in some part of the making process themselves, and many have some shop-floor experience of most of the crafts they're supervising. The freelance maker working at home will usually only have contact with the designer at the start of the job, when they go through the designs and discuss what's required, and then at costume fittings; otherwise they'll be in touch by telephone. Any queries about materials, delivery dates, fees and so on, are made through the designer's assistant or the head of department of the company concerned.

An important time for the maker is during the final setting up of a theatre or opera production, a week or so before opening night. The maker will aim to arrive at the theatre with the work 90 per cent complete, and the designer, in co-operation with the director, choreographer and whomever, will 'pull' everything together visually, and iron out any technical problems ('I can't do cartwheels in this headdress,' etc.) by seeing all the work on stage during the final rehearsals. He or she will recommend painting and spraying here, some adding of braid there, and so on. These are exciting, adrenalin-fuelled days (and nights) when the corporate effort of many craftspeople becomes one whole.

A large, lavish opera production may use, in addition to its permanent staff: men and women principals' costumiers; an animal costumier; a men's hat-maker; a women's hat-maker; a helmet and fancy headdress maker; an armourer; wig-makers; a mask-maker; a make-up adviser (for something special like painted bodies); a small props maker (spears, etc.); a large props maker (statues, etc.); a specialist in costume painting, dyeing and breaking down (ageing). In addition to these, a prop-maker may be called in to decorate boots and shoes, or a milliner engaged just to make flowers for the set – there's always a certain overlapping of skills, especially when a great number of arcane objects are required. The costumiers are likely to have one or more full-time assistants, and during busy periods other craftspeople may have help from a student or young acquaintance interested in entering the business. It's unlikely that many freelance people will have enough work, or income, to employ a full-time apprentice, although in some cases this is badly needed in order to perpetuate skills.

These few days in the theatre are when the outworker meets her colleagues, catches up on gossip, shares technical tips, hears about company vacancies or gaps in freelance skills. There's a lot of camaraderie, and a certain amount of furtive looking inside costumes or at the structure of the props – it's not exactly poaching, but one of the few ways an outworker can improve her technique and enlarge her skill, once she's on her own.

When all the work is finished and the show goes on, the designer and makers depart feeling exhausted, somewhat anti-climactic and marginal-ised, as then the performers take the applause. It's an emotionally draining profession with a vaguely 'below stairs' status. Makers are not often invited to opening night parties. At some point in their career, most makers will reflect on the parties they missed or the film they failed to catch because they stayed up all night making a headdress for a show which they and the public have forgotten. They will wonder if anyone noticed the headdress, and if the whole business is at all worthwhile. However, it's a compulsive occupation: the next job is interesting, and it's wanted next week.

British film executives and media movie buffs are often heard bemoaning the government's reluctance to recognise and promote the potential of their growth industry. If they were to mention that for everyone whose name appears on the credit list there are a dozen whose names don't, perhaps we might have a better idea of the scale of the business and the true economic implications. Like so much of the other work in our society, a great deal of theatrical making is done by women, and is hidden.

Barley Roscoe

ARTIST CRAFTSWOMEN BETWEEN THE WARS

Barley Roscoe writes here about the sales outlets –
the galleries, exhibitions and the patrons – of some of
the more successful women craftworkers of the
1920s and '30s.

Few of the leading artist craftswomen working in the
years immediately following the First World War had to live entirely on
what they earned. Many had some private means to help them and came
from well-to-do families. These emancipated middle-class women, having
elected the crafts as a respectable occupation at which to earn a living
(either as a practitioner or entrepreneur), may often be regarded as
pioneers within their chosen field. The talent of various notable figures,
and the revival of interest in the crafts generally during the 1920s, meant
that by the 1930s not only was their position better established in society,
but there were also recognised channels for the sale of their work which
in turn helped to promote them.

In particular three commercial London galleries played an important
part in this development. The first to open, in 1922, was the Three Shields
Gallery at 8 Holland Street, just off Kensington High Street. This was the
brainchild of Dorothy Hutton who had formerly studied at the Central
School of Art and had already established her reputation as a calligrapher
with various commissions including some for the royal family. Displays in
the gallery concentrated on lithographs, drawings, watercolours, prints
and some tempera paintings; while pottery, textiles and silverware were
also shown as changing exhibitions that usually lasted about three weeks.
Bernard Leach and Michael Cardew were amongst the potters whose
work was displayed, and during the early 1920s Phyllis Barron and Dorothy
Larcher also had exhibitions of their hand-block printed textiles there.
These two, though they had trained as painters, shared a textile print
studio in Hampstead at the time, where they were later also joined by
the designer Enid Marx. For a time the weaver Ethel Mairet hired a room
in the gallery for up to a fortnight twice a year to show her work. For a

THE LITTLE GALLERY

M. Rose   M. K. Turnbull

ELLIS STREET, *turning off*
SLOANE ST., S.W.1

Sloane 6663

The New Handworkers

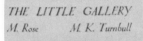

14 Percy Street W

FURNITURE. WOVEN GOODS.
PRINTED TEXTILES AND POTTERY.
METAL AND OTHER HAND-WORK
BY EMINENT CRAFTSMEN.

OPEN DAILY 10
NEAREST
GOODGE STREET
CO
TELEPHON

The Leach Pottery S.t Ives. Cornwall.
In ½c with New P

The New
Handworkers
Gallery 6 Fitzroy

PERMANENT exhibition
Crafts, by the following Craf
men and others:—

BLOCKPRINTED FABRICS
  Phyllis Barron and
  Dorothy Larcher
FURNITURE
  A. Romney Green a
  Stanley Davies
METAL WORK
  Fredk. J. Partridge a
  G. Hart
POTTERY
  Bernard Leach and
  Michael Cardew
PRINTING
  St. Dominic's Press
WEAVING
  Ethel M. Mairet

Hours:
Daily: 10 to 6. Saturday: 10 to
Closed between 1 and 2

BARRON AND LARCHER

Hand-printed Stuffs for summer dresses
in new designs are being shewn specially

DURING THE MONTH OF MAY
AT THE LITTLE GALLERY
3 ELLIS ST: SLOANE ST: S.W.1

A small collection of early printed cottons and
printing blocks from different countries are
included in this exhibition, as well as some of
the blocks used at the present time by Barron
and Larcher at Hambutts House, Painswick,
Gloucestershire.

The honour of your company is requested at

AN EXHIBITION OF
OLD FRENCH & ENGLISH
COTTON PRINTS

Collected by
PHYLLIS BARRON &
DOROTHY LARCHER

The majority of the pieces exhibited
are not for sale

THE LITTLE GALLERY
5 ELLIS STREET off SLOANE ST., S.W.1

Wednesday, April 23 to Saturday, May 10

The New Handwor
Gallery 6 Fitzroy Square

E. Mairet & G. Norsworthy   Fi

PHYLLIS BARRO
DOROTHY LARCHE
INVITE YOU TO SEE THE
EXHIBITION OF HAND PRINT
STUFFS. APRIL 25 TO MA
10-6. SATURDAYS 10-1 AT T
LITTLE GALLER
3 ELLIS STREE
SLOANE ST: S.W

Private view cards and gallery information from the 1920s

Sadler

Telephone Fitzroy 1464

The New Handworkers Gallery
14 Percy Street, W.1

PERMANENT EXHIBITION BY INDIVIDUAL CRAFTSMEN IN-
CLUDING PHYLLIS BARRON, MICHAEL CARDEW, BERNARD
LEACH, ROMNEY GREEN AND ETHEL MAIRET.

Philippe Mairet.   *Nearest Tube Station:*
Evelyn Cooper.   *Mar. 12.*   *Goodge St. Tottenham Ct. Rd.*

0

...workers' Pamphlets   No. 4
1s. od.

Art and
Manufacture

ERIC GILL

/ HANDWORKERS' GALLERY

HANDWORKERS' PAMPHLETS

No. 1. The Idea Behind Craftsmanship
by Philippe Mairet

(Out of print)

No. 2. Instead of a Catalogue
by A. Romney Green
The Apologia of a Furniture Maker

No. 3. A Potter's Outlook
by Bernard Leach

No. 4. Art and Manufacture
by Eric Gill

OTHERS IN PREPARATION

: LITTLE GALLERY
STREET, SLOANE STREET, S.W.

MONDAY, 8th NOV.
to
ATURDAY, 20th NOV.

'HEL MAIRET

DWOVEN TWEEDS, SCARFS,
SHIONS, CURTAINS, ETC.

ing, Sussex

PHYLLIS BARRON
DOROTHY LARCHER

invite you to see their block printed stuffs for
summer dresses and furnishing. There will also
be a large selection of scarves in new designs.

IN THE MONTH
OF MAY AT THE

LITTLE GALLERY
3 ELLIS STREET
SLOANE ST: S.W.1

Visitors to the Cotswolds are always welcomed
at Hambutts House Painswick Gloucestershire

brief spell in the early 1930s, after the closure of her own New Handworkers' Gallery, she regarded the Three Shields as her London base and
arranged to be there one day each week to meet clients.

Two young women were employed to help Dorothy Hutton in the
gallery as she wished to do her own creative work and didn't want to be
tied to being on the premises all the time. Muriel Rose joined her early
on (in her first paid job), and worked as her assistant for five years. There
she met Peggy Turnbull, who did the accounts for the gallery a couple of
days each week, and the two decided to go into partnership with some
£1,000 between them. It took nearly a year to find inexpensive but
suitable premises with plenty of daylight, but finally they discovered a
former laundry depot in Ellis Street, just off Sloane Square. It consisted of
one large room on the ground floor with windows at both front and back
plus a good skylight and an adequate basement below. They converted
the space as best they could with the minimum of expense by stripping it
inside to make it as plain as possible and using a good deal of white paint.
In subsequent years they expanded into neighbouring premises.

A notice of the Little Gallery's opening in *The Times* of 9 October 1928
recorded that the aim appeared:

> to be to keep a stock of the less expensive productions of
> handicraft and the more artistically considered wares of the
> factory, and a word is due to the consistently high quality
> maintained in this modest range. Everything is on the side of
> reticence, the designs being simple and the colours inclining to
> 'secondaries' and 'tertiaries' in subtle combinations.

From the start Muriel Rose decided to exhibit only the best craftwork she
could find. She was determined that the gallery should not be an 'omnium
gatherum', nor resemble a gift shop. She was also anxious not to compete
with the Three Shields Gallery by showing things that Dorothy Hutton
stocked. She had first seen and admired the work of Barron and Larcher
at a Christmas exhibition there and, knowing that Hutton didn't keep their
work permanently, felt able to approach them. This was the start of a
long and lasting friendship, and after Barron and Larcher moved to
Painswick from Hampstead in 1930 the Little Gallery became their main
London sales outlet for the decade. Although their materials were held
in stock, special summer and Christmas exhibitions of their work were
arranged as well. Pottery exhibitions at the Little Gallery included work
by Bernard Leach and Michael Cardew. Katharine Pleydell-Bouverie and
Norah Braden exhibited there – in fact, the wood-fired, ash-glazed
stoneware these women made at Coleshill was the subject of the first of
the gallery's shows. Other stocked items included silverware by Catherine
Cockerell and decorative printed papers designed by Enid Marx – both
French marbled and Japanese papers used for bookbinding – along with
Welsh quilts and some furniture. The gallery showed weaving by Dorothy
Kemp, table linen by Rita and Percy Beales, lengths from Ethel Mairet's

The weaving room at Gospels in the early 1920s

workshop and woven work by Elizabeth Peacock. The latter held a highly successful exhibition and demonstration there in 1938, visited by numerous students and schoolchildren.

Occasionally, Ethel Mairet would arrange to have a show at the gallery. She had her own cards printed to let her clients know she would be there, and on the specified day she would arrive in a taxi from Victoria with the materials in a number of holdalls. Then, in a flurry of activity, she would hang them up in a rather slapdash way so that within an hour she would be ready to receive clients. This followed the ending of her arrangement with Dorothy Hutton and the closure in 1931 of the New Handworkers' Gallery, which she had started up under the name of her second husband Philip Mairet at roughly the same time as the Little Gallery. The letter heading announced that it had a 'Permanent exhibition by individual craftsmen including Phyllis Barron, Michael Cardew, Bernard Leach, Romney Green and Ethel Mairet'. Work by other craftswomen – including pottery by Pleydell-Bouverie and Braden, and lampshades made from printed papers by Enid Marx – were also shown, although there was some discussion amongst the 'regulars' as to whether non-permanent exhibitors' work should be included.

The New Handworkers' Gallery proved a profitable sales outlet for some members for a short period, but it was never really a flourishing concern. PAM (as Philip Mairet was sometimes known) could not be described as a businessman – he was usually too busy writing for *The New Age* or editing pamphlets to notice whether a visitor needed encouragement to make a purchase. And the position, the first floor of 14 Percy Street, near the Tottenham Court Road, was not auspicious. The move to a better location at 6 Fitzroy Square in 1930 seemed promising, and the gallery was now advertised as being run by Ethel Mairet and Gwendoline Norsworthy. However, the gallery swiftly closed when Ethel Mairet discovered PAM and Mrs Norsworthy to be having an affair.

These galleries were valuable sales outlets; the Little Gallery, in particular, fostered a select and wealthy clientele which included titled patrons. In general, work was stocked on a sale or return basis and a commission of 33 per cent commission was taken. In addition, the gallery owners were often instrumental in obtaining commissions for the work of these craftswomen, as shown by the full correspondence between Mairet and members of the New Handworkers' Gallery, or by the friendly letters between Muriel Rose and Barron and Larcher during the 1930s. Here, details of orders are interspersed with day-to-day news such as 'Miss Edsall is telling us about Lady Ludlow's eight Peke dogs who have leather boots put on by the footman before they come into the drawing room.'[1] Apart from direct commissions entered in Barron and Larcher's order book for 1938–45, orders from the Little Gallery in Muriel Rose's handwriting are pinned into the book, often with special instructions: 'Printed in the nearest you can do to a coral colour *not* browny!' or 'By Tuesday next without fail.'[2]

Both their order book, and that of Enid Marx (1937), show a fairly even mix of titled patrons, craftsmen and women, and supporters. Lady Alice Reyntiens, Lady Debenham, Lady Adare and Lady Loch are all recorded as ordering Barron and Larcher materials, together with notable figures in the craft world such as Gordon Russell, Eric Sharpe, Ernest Gimson's widow and the Elmhirsts. Commissions varied from a headscarf to considerable yardage for upholstery or curtaining: two of the more important orders during the 1930s were for curtains for the Senior Common Room in Girton College, Cambridge, and for the choir stalls at Winchester Cathedral. Some of the most lucrative orders were from the Duke of Westminster, whose commissions to Barron and Larcher included refurbishing his estate office in Davies Street for his daughter's coming-out dance, doing up his hunting lodge in Bordeaux, and printing all the upholstery and curtaining for *The Flying Cloud*, his Elizabethan-style yacht, which required materials for 'forty cabins, each with divans, bunks and curtains, and an enormous saloon in the middle'. Initially, Barron was given only three weeks to fulfil this order, and enlisted the help of friends to print all day and recut blocks at night. However, after three weeks, they

> still hadn't done a quarter of the job and should never have
> satisfied the Duke's whim – for he wanted any new toy at
> once – had not a boilermakers' strike intervened. For the Duke,
> although he wanted all the picturesqueness of sailing, didn't
> want the ship becalmed, and was having engines fitted.

Fortunately for Barron, the strike lasted three months and this meant the job could be completed 'even to the cushions'.[3]

Dorothy and Leonard Elmhirst, who founded Dartington Hall in 1925, were particularly enlightened and munificent patrons. Their community was centred on concepts of a renewed countryside, re-employment, liberty of intellect, technical competence, a rediscovery of the right place for the arts and a fuller recognition of children's potential. It was the Elmhirsts who gave the weaver Elizabeth Peacock one of her most important commissions – 'six, then eight, later ten, large heraldic-like banners to solve the acoustic problems of using Dartington's fourteenth-century hall for music'.[4] During the 1920s Peacock's commissions ranged from 'all the material to furnish particular flats in Paris, and a steady stream of dress lengths and stoles for Schiaparelli', to a stole for King Feisal of Iraq, a connoisseur of cotton.

Exhibitions at which stands were rented by exhibitors also proved popular sales outlets. Standards and quality were apt to vary. The Englishwoman Exhibition of Arts and Handicrafts was one of the first, started in 1910 in connection with *The Englishwoman* magazine. It was held every November in the Central Hall, Westminster, for ten days. Phyllis Barron took a stall but found it to be

> a rather terrible sort of Christmas bazaar ... a lady next door
> to me sold brooches made of fishbones, and one on the other
> side decorated jam jars with oil paint. Mrs Mairet was
> somewhere right across the Hall, and I felt very lost and had to
> console myself with Guinness...[5]

But 'several people remember the impact made in 1923 by four outstanding, dignified women – impressive as personalities and as artists – who

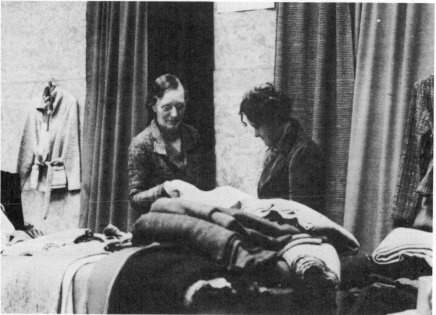

Ethel Mairet at the Red Rose Guild Exhibition, c. 1938

each had stalls.' The four were Jean Orage, rug weaver; Ethel Mairet; Phyllis Barron, and Elizabeth Peacock 'looking lovely in a cochineal wool dress of her own spinning'.[6] In contrast, the exhibitions of the Arts and Crafts Exhibition Society (founded in 1888) which showed at the Royal Academy, Burlington House, upheld standards rigorously and the work was chosen by a selection committee.

The Guild of Weavers, Spinners and Dyers was founded in 1931 and their first exhibition at the Whitechapel Art Gallery in 1935 proved a momentous occasion. Apart from members' own stands (Beales, Peacock and Ethel Mairet's workshop), this ambitious show also displayed weaving by students at art school and 'hand weaving by factory designers and factory woven stuffs designed on hand looms', with some textiles by Marianne Straub.[7] Other allied crafts were included, with block prints by Barron, Larcher and Marx, and embroidery by Eve Simmonds.

The Red Rose Guild of Artworkers at Manchester started in January 1921 and held its exhibition each autumn until the Second World War. The Arts and Crafts Year Book of 1926 records that

> owing to the interest taken by the members in the improvement and organisation of their exhibition ... bazaar stalls have been replaced by stalls specially made to fit in under the gallery [in the Houldsworth Hall, Deansgate] and ... a general colour scheme was introduced of cream outlined with black and gold which proved an excellent background for the exhibits.

Although the most responsible girls from Ethel Mairet's workshop were trusted to hold the stand at the London exhibitions, Ethel Mairet always tried to go to the Red Rose Guild exhibitions herself. Other female exhibitors included Dorothy Kemp, Kathleen Heron, Phyllis Barron and Dorothy Larcher, and Katharine Pleydell-Bouverie.

Most of these craftswomen would also sell from their own workshops. However, Rita Beales emphasised that 'We never advertised and we never put up at the gate "Weavers" – you can't work with people coming in and out, it upsets your day completely!'[8] In general, sales were made mostly to those 'in the know' rather than passing trade. A system Barron and Larcher adopted when living in Painswick was to have small exhibitions of their work from time to time. Ethel Mairet went a step further and after the closure of the New Handworkers' Gallery opened her own shop in Brighton at 68a East Street. It proved a successful venture and was in existence for nearly two decades.

Galleries, exhibitions and patrons all played an important role in helping to promote the crafts in the interwar years, and the craftswomen mentioned utilised them all to a greater or lesser degree as the means by which to sell their work and make their reputations. But only the principal sales outlets for a comparatively small group of women have been mentioned here, representing only a part of the complete picture for the period.

BARRON, Phyllis (1890-1964)
Hand-block printed textile designer. Studied painting under Tonks and Steer, Slade School of Art, London. Mainly self-taught in textile design from 1915. Established textile printing studio in Hampstead, London, joined by Dorothy Larcher c.1923. Workshop in Painswick, Gloucestershire, 1930-40.

BEALES, Rita (née Rabone) (1889-   )
Came to England from New Zealand on a scholarship to the Royal College of Music, London; studied opera singing. In 1917 married Percy Beales (d. 1963). Mainly self-taught in weaving from 1918. Established weaving workshop and concentrated on linen and wool weaving at Lopham, Norfolk, 1926-35; Compton Chamberlayne, Wiltshire, 1935-8; Cerney Wick, Gloucestershire, 1938-60; Daneway, Gloucestershire, 1960-66; Painswick, Gloucestershire, from 1966.

BRADEN, Norah (1901-   )
Potter. Studied drawing at the Central School of Arts and Crafts, London, and the violin at Trinity College of Music, London. Subsequently studied painting at the Royal College of Art. Joined Bernard Leach as a student at his pottery in St Ives 1925-6. Worked with Katharine Pleydell-Bouverie at Coleshill, Berkshire, for periods in 1928-36. Taught pottery part-time

at Brighton College of Art 1936-9, 1945-50; at Bishop Otter College, Chichester, 1945-66, and at Camberwell College of Art 1950-55. Taught pottery full-time at Chichester College of Further Education 1966-7.

LARCHER, Dorothy (1884-1952)
Hand-block printed textile designer and artist. Studied painting at Hornsey College of Art. Joined Phyllis Barron c. 1923 and worked at textile printing studio in Hampstead, London, until 1930, and then Painswick, Gloucestershire, 1930-40. Concentrated on painting at Painswick 1939-52.

MAIRET, Ethel (née Partridge) RDI (1872-1952)
Weaver. Attended the Municipal Science and Art Schools, Barnstaple. Married Ananda Coomaraswamy in 1902 and lived in Ceylon 1903-6; Broad Campden, Gloucestershire, 1907-10. Following divorce in 1910, married Philip Mairet 1913 (separated 1931). Mainly self-taught in weaving from 1909, concentrated on weaving at Saunton Sands 1911-13; established workshop at Shottery 1913-18. Moved to Ditchling, Sussex, 1918 and built 'Gospels' Workshop, established 1920-52, attended by English and foreign weavers and students. Opened New Handworkers' Gallery 1927-31, and shop in Brighton 1934-c.1951. Taught weaving at Brighton College of Art 1939-47. Published books on vegetable dyeing, handweaving and education.

MARX, Enid RDI (1902-   )
Designer. Studied drawing, pottery and textile design under Bernard Adeney, Central School of Arts and Crafts, London, and went on to study painting and wood engraving at the Royal College of Art. Joined Barron and Larcher's workshop 1925-7. Established own textile printing studio in Hampstead in 1927, later moved to St John's Wood. Became a member of the Board of Trade Utility Furniture Panel, designing for woven textiles, laminates and PVC plastic. Has also designed moquettes for London Transport in addition to book jackets, pattern papers and stamps. Head of Dress, Textiles and Pottery at Croydon College of Art 1960-65. Written and illustrated many children's books, co-author of *English Popular Art* (Batsford, 1951).

PEACOCK, Elizabeth (1880-1969)
Weaver. Studied painting at Birmingham School of Art. In 1917 joined Ethel Mairet in handweaving workshop at Stratford-on-Avon and subsequently moved with her to Ditchling, Sussex. Established own workshop with Molly Stobart at Clayton, Sussex, 1922-69. Co-founder of first Guild of Weavers, Spinners and Dyers 1931. Taught weaving part-time at Reigate and Redhill School of Art 1940-57.

PLEYDELL-BOUVERIE, Katharine (1895-1985)
Potter. Studied ceramics at the Central School of Arts and Crafts, London. Joined Bernard Leach as a student at his pottery in St Ives 1924-5.

Established pottery at Coleshill, Berkshire, and concentrated on experimenting with wood and vegetable ash-glazes 1925-40, joined by Norah Braden 1928-36. Moved to Kilmington and established pottery 1946-85.

Sara Bowman

EMBROIDERERS AT HOME
Women of the Sixty-Two Group

Sara Bowman talks to three embroiderers who
are all members of the Sixty-Two Group, which is
concerned with the promotion of embroidery as an
art form. These women are not privileged in the
same sense as many of those in the 1920s and '30s,
and are frequently dependent on other income (their
own or a spouse's) to support their craftwork.

Since the 1850s professional and amateur groups have
been formed to promote the art of stitchery. The most vigorous of these
is now the pioneer Sixty-Two Group, founded in November 1962 by a
few embroiderers who worked largely outside the mainstream. The
group's formation was prompted by the lack of available venues for those
working creatively with embroidery and textiles at the time. Founder
members Alison Lilley, Jennifer Gray and Joy Clucas sought, by way of
exhibitions, to expose new aspects of embroidery and textiles. From the
outset the group adopted a rigorous selection policy; today, membership
is by selection and contribution to group exhibitions. 'The group does not
have a dogmatic policy or manifesto, but encourages members to develop
their own ideas according to their vision. What holds the group together
is the conviction that in working with textiles and thread the artist inherits
a rich tradition of techniques and materials that is unique in the visual
arts.'[1]

There are sixty-six members throughout the country. Informal meetings,
seminars and discussions take place both nationally and regionally. A
newsletter links and informs members. Regular exhibitions act as a show-
case for new developments in the textile arts. From its inception the
Sixty-Two Group has sought to forge links with industrial design and
production, though so far these links have not been very strong and work
for the future must include renewed energy in this direction. Education
has been seen as a priority and some members of the group hold key
teaching posts, contributing to research and publications. Today women

textile artists are challenging the subversive role that practitioners of the past had to accept; they are actively seeking public exposure and recognition of their work as a valid art form.

Barbara Siedlecka is a long-standing member of the Sixty-Two Group. Barbara works from home and her studio is a small room which looks out on to the landscaped gardens of a London suburb. She divides her time between working to commission, co-ordinating the Beckenham Studios, part-time teaching and her own stitchery and illustration work.

'At college I studied illustration because it was the nearest I could get to pure drawing. Drawing was then, and still is, my most direct means of expression. This was just after the war. We studied anatomy and perspective, and we drew from the antique and from life, every day. In order to secure an art school job in the fifties, I studied "women's crafts" at art college – weaving, embroidery, pattern-cutting and dress-design – in addition to my drawing and painting. I can't really remember how I learnt to sew in the first place, but I know my mother taught me, like learning to use a knife and fork, I suppose.

'I then worked as an art editor and illustrator and it wasn't until fifteen years later that I turned once more to fabric and thread. I had been experimenting with colour etching – the richly textured and embossed

Barbara Siedlecka with a painted suede collage

KENTISH TIMES

surfaces were like brocades – and it seemed a natural progression to move into textiles. I joined the Beckenham Studios of which I am now organiser. We're a group of art school trained women working in similar media, and we meet weekly for discussion and mutual support. We exhibit together as well; and this, together with my membership of the Sixty-Two Group, provides me with the opportunity to show my personal work. I embroider, and I see it very much as an extension of drawing; the same thought processes are involved, the same concerns of contour, volume, weight, stress, tension. It's not a question of embroidering a drawing, but of using the information acquired through drawing. I don't find it possible to do a little every day. I have first to think around an idea, let it mature. Then I draw and draw, to clarify the image; when I'm ready I work at it non-stop till it's finished. That's the luxury of working for myself. The deadline is provided by an exhibition, otherwise this personal work could go on indefinitely, evolving and changing direction. It might be interesting to allow a piece to continue developing sometimes, but then I also admire efficiency and the getting of things done, so I should be unlikely to let that happen.

'It is commonly thought that working to commision is inhibiting, but I've found the reverse to be the case. I like the challenge of problem-solving within the time available. New ideas and techniques evolve through necessity and are then ready to be exploited in the next personal piece. For example I've worked on some large architectural commissions where the challenge of scale has forced me to produce works very much akin to mural painting. These are at once an extension of the architectural perspectives I used to draw, and also lead into a personal kind of work composed of architectural elements and enclosed spaces which attempt to create an atmosphere of place from my own experience. Teaching is important for me too, for personal contact, but it's crucial to keep a proper balance. Presently I feel I have that, with each of my activities complementing the other.'

Julia Caprara is a textile artist, freelance fashion embroiderer, part-time teacher and chairperson of the Sixty-Two Group. She works at home with stitchery, making rich and detailed wall-hangings which carry poignant messages. The most recent work reflects her concern for world peace.

'Like other women of my generation, I took time to discover and then explore the potential of stitchery. As an art student in the fifties, opportunities for work with textiles were rare. Initially I studied stained glass and wood-engraving and intended developing my work in terms of paint or sculpture. I then discovered textiles and embroidery as expressive media and a woman friend guided me to an embroidery class at The London College of Fashion. I found that for me textiles were an effective way of making statements, and I acquired further skills informally from friends and colleagues.

MICHEL MOLINARE

Julia Caprara with one of her fabric collages, 'There is no Garden at Babiy Yar', one of her first political pieces. She uses both collage and stitching techniques

SARA BOWMAN

Elaine Waller at work

'My early work was about myths and legends. I took themes from the Greek myths and from the Book of Revelations and translated them into wall-hangings. I later became interested in textural assemblages in terms of landscape, building detailed fragments into large textural surfaces. Embroidery is a superb medium for landscape because certain stitch qualities have parallels in nature. At first I worked with any materials to hand – darning or knitting wool, pieces of scrim – and since my knowledge of stitchery was so limited, I used the simplest methods, such as running, tent and back stitch, and I still do. More recently – since recovering from a serious illness – my work has been influenced by my feelings about pain; I've wanted to express something about our inner strengths. These new works are different in that they're making political statements as, for example, my *Peace Mandala*. I like using contrasting qualities together, such as silk with hessian, paper with metal. I work with materials from my immediate environment, both natural and 'man-made' and I use both hand and machine stitchery.

'From the very beginning of my involvement with stitchery I was able to show my work with groups and to benefit from the pioneer work of women like Constance Howard, who had helped set up the New Embroidery Group in the sixties. My membership of the Sixty-Two Group has helped stretch my professionalism, too; I work because I need to communicate, and regular discussions and exhibitions complete a cycle. I set aside time each day for work and usually have four or five pieces in progress. Many of my teaching samplers become working drawings for my own work. But I do think that many of us working at home are very isolated, and the cloistered life may do us a disservice. The opportunity to meet with others, working similarly, I've found to be a valuable support network.'

Elaine Waller works at home making embroidered pictures. Textile printer, Karen Harrison, describes her work:

> Tiny, intricate embroideries of circus animals, performers, clowns and dancers, they have an ethereal quality, and light on the silky threads seems to make the figures move, their expressions change. She successfully creates a sense of depth and space that I haven't seen in embroidery before. Looking at her work is like seeing a fairy story come alive and step on to the table beside you.[2]

Some of her work makes pertinent comment on the state of the world – executed in fine stitchery, they shock and haunt.

Elaine says, 'My interest in embroidery evolved out of my interest in weaving, story-telling and illustration. I had a formal art school education; I studied weaving at Winchester College and then Fine Art Textiles at Goldsmith's. My use of embroidery is something like writing a diary; each picture is a reflection of a moment when I saw an image, it records the effect the image had on me. Usually I make a quick black and white sketch for the piece and then work straight on to the fabric, allowing the embroidery to evolve naturally. For me embroidery embodies the quiet, unknown self, the subconscious, so I sometimes feel the pictures dictate their own stories. Often their meaning is not fully known to me. The materials that I use to embroider on are integral to the stitches, and these develop differently for each picture too, so that both are enmeshed. I use thin muslin, old silk, rotten pieces of fine material and even tissue paper. Employing a variety of stitches, including French knots and running stitches, on fabrics that are unhemmed and uncut, I always work without a frame and never use a machine; I enjoy the slowness of hand embroidery, and its freedom.

'Since leaving college I've worked on my embroidery from a corner of my bedroom, though recently I've felt a need to become involved with a medium which is less isolating and I've joined with a small group of puppeteers. We write and perform with shadow puppets and I've found these activities complement each other – the scale of each is a contrast. I like joint artistic projects and I'd like to join in work with other embroiderers too.'

From these interviews some common threads emerge. Members of the group, like many textile artists, work from home; here the overheads are low and domestic commitments may be met; their workspace is often a modest room, a corner of the bedroom or the kitchen table. Women's working time has always been fragmented as a result of domestic arrangements, and many textile artists have used this positively to develop diversification in their work; some combine their art practice with more immediately communicative activities such as teaching, some have explored alternative ways of collaborating with other women on joint artistic projects. Both formal professional groups and informal women's networks are crucial – to overcome isolation, to give support and the opportunity of exposure and criticism.

Jane Kennard

MONEY AND SUCCESS
Markets for jewellery

'I'd be ashamed to say what I earn,' says jeweller
Jane Kennard, and she reiterates the fact that most
craftworkers need to subsidise their pleasure in
work. 'It's time for some success,' she says, after
seven years of craftwork that has 'ticked over quite
nicely'.

I came to Birmingham from Cardiff for a degree in
jewellery design. I followed that up with postgraduate research in design
history, then I had the chance to join two other jewellers in a barn of a
craft workshop, literally, run by Redditch Development Corporation
outside Birmingham. The place was much too big and freezing cold; we
had to rewire it and, for me, the travelling was heavy. We each bought
equipment to share between ourselves. I worked there for about eighteen
months, doing my basic professional learning in the company of others,
though we none of us knew much about marketing or business practice.
I was better off than most because my parents had run a business in which
I'd had some experience, so I knew about invoices and order books and
I'd kept accounts. I remember showing the man I worked with how to
write a cheque because he'd never had a.bank account.

I had very little money; I'd been able to put only £100 into my business,
so it was very difficult to make any return back. I was actually living on
part-time adult education teaching. When money was really short, I
worked as a 'John Player Girl' on cigarette promotion, and other jobs,
then injected the cash straight back into the business. At this time, sale or
return was the commonest way of trade, but it didn't pay off. When a
friend opened a jewellery shop and workshop, I decided to work with
her for two or three days a week. The wages were low but I learnt a
great deal. Di was experienced and helped me with the technical things I
hadn't been taught at college, such as how to finish work in a professional
way. Just as there was little instruction on business practice at my college,
no one there had worried about what would happen if you actually sold
a piece, like would it stay in one piece, or fall apart? I think they

thought they were training just designers there, ones with strong fine art orientations, though there could never be enough patrons to support all the jewellers coming out of college. Anyway, Di showed me where to get findings (rings, clips and wires, used to hold pieces together) and she showed me how to use the casting process properly, which was essential for repeat production. I also learned how to talk to customers in a professional way.

I worked at the shop with Di for two years. It overlapped with the Redditch Centre, but I was finding that journey too much, especially if I wanted to work at night. It was an isolated place, unpleasant after dark and a bit spooky. So I moved my workshop into my flat. I still work from home, but I do worry that I won't be taken seriously because of it. You know, the idea that if it's at home, and you're a woman, it can't be a real business. There's another myth too, that jewellery is neat, clean and nice, like the end product, and like a certain image of women. In fact it's filthy, physical work, and it's hard on the hands. To get that nice, delicate little piece of jewellery, I have to bash metal with a ten pound hammer.

At about the time I moved my workshop, an ex-tutor from Birmingham told me about the Designer Jewellers' Group which exists to exhibit as a group at trade fairs. She introduced me to the group, which I now chair after seven years of working with them. She also introduced me to a group of mixed craft designers called Design Gap. Together these groups led me into professional selling. I first took £100 worth of space on a large stand at the National Exhibition Centre, with other jewellers. Gradually I produced a small range of silver and resin work which was unusual at the time, and still sells. It's ticked over quite nicely but I've never made it really big because it's a small market. I've never wanted to travel round with my work to sell it. I prefer selling to people who've already shown an interest, and will re-order. I like to establish a contact and a base, and know I have a good stockist I can publicise. I work through trade shows – that way I can reach people all over the country from one base. It's ideal for work that can be repeated like mine. Travelling around to sell can be quite lucrative for a limited range of one-off pieces that are constantly changed. It doesn't work for the kind of fashion jewellery I do. I couldn't let several shops in the same town have my jewellery range – they'd all price it differently and it would be I who got the customers' complaints. Added to that, there would be no exclusivity for the shops, unless they had a really huge turnover, so I don't let my work go into more than one shop in an area.

I concentrated on a fashion jewellery range in plastics and after a while I had work accepted by the Design Centre, and found that I was able to stand on my own two financial feet. I pay the Design Council each year for their services, to have my name on their register. Through them I've sold a lot of work in the shop, they've promoted my work abroad, and I have my work in their magazine from time to time. I keep them informed

Jane Kennard, jeweller

ANDREW SARGENT

and they use the information; it works. Other shops take their lead from the Design Centre, so if you're in, you're okay – otherwise there's no door, just a brick wall. I used to believe that the Crafts Council (and the Design Centre) were very elitist, but now I think, if you can't beat them, join them; those who have are doing very well. It involves so much paperwork and before I had always been too busy trying to keep my head above water to apply to them.

I now consider myself a professional jeweller and designer, though I subsidise my business through teaching on top of my full-time craft work. Most people I know who had six years in college and seven years out are earning a fair whack, and I'd be ashamed to say what I earn! I think this not only goes for jewellers but for most craftspeople. I know some quite successful craftworkers, for example some potters who have a workshop; they have work in the Design Centre and have been covered by the magazines, and they still produce all the work themselves. But they can no longer compete without employing people, something they are unwilling to do. Who wants a factory and employees? Of the hundred or so working jewellers I know, only one actually designs for a company, the work we were originally trained for. I know one or two others who sell designs from time to time, or who have worked for large firms like Cartiers for a pittance, but not for long because the money is so poor. Some work with Crafts Council backing, but these fortunate ones are few and tend to stay the same year after year. In the West Midlands, Arts Council grants are only given for community linked projects; if you live in Sussex, or in other areas, you can get an equipment grant. A friend in Kent has had grant aid for equipment that it's taken me seven years of work to acquire.

Most jewellers work part-time to subsidise their jewellery. Many of them are women (hobbyists), who sell their work for much less than its value; this particularly gets me down because it undervalues all jewellery. Then there are the handful like myself, who work at the craft full-time, but still need to subsidise it. You have to put in a large amount of capital to get large returns; I used to think hard work would do it, but it doesn't. You need expensive coloured brochures and good equipment; the right things at the right time, not two years later, because by then you've missed your chance. Someone else will step in who's younger and brighter and fresher; they'll have time to develop while you're tied up with hand-to-mouth making and selling.

Unfortunately, it's taken me these seven years to realise that I've been pitching my work all wrong. It's been a total lack of foresight and planning on my part. I didn't think that I had any choice about how I worked; I just assumed that it all happened, but it doesn't. You have to make policy decisions and stick to them. Here I am making hand-made stuff in what should be a mass-produced market. I need to turn over large amounts of cheap pieces, and I can't do that by hand. My work needs to be more mechanised and I need to design for processes, so that some of the work

JOËL DEGEN

Examples of Jane Kennard's jewellery. Bold geometric shapes cut from flat sheet plastic are engraved with patterns which are inlaid with brightly coloured resins

can be done by someone else. I've spent seven years making this stuff, and if I got £40,000 worth of orders tomorrow, I'd die, because I'd have to make them all! What would be bliss now would be to design one-offs, even in plastics, but different every day. But that won't happen unless I rethink and approach the work in a different way. It should be possible for me to design just for processes, producing work that is as good and interesting as I am now, but which I wouldn't need to handle right through. But for that I need time to investigate the market and the costings, and I need to push the techniques to their limits. And, of course, I'll have to finance myself with some other work in order to put it all into practice. Then, if the £40,000 order did come in, I'd welcome it. I love travelling, I love designing, I love selling, but I hate this repetitive work, and I'm not going to do it any more.

I've had a few big opportunities lately. I've been to New York and Hong Kong this year, and learned that there is a market abroad. Fortunately, changes in fashion don't affect me too much; my work is geared to a middle market, but it is a very narrow field here. There is just about enough work across the country. I think I now have an American agent from the New York trip, and my work will be shown there soon. I need to follow up the Hong Kong contacts with professional brochures; it could be a long-term thing with Japanese orders from department stores, and so on. It will all need a year to follow through, then, if the orders are big enough, I can transfer my processes into laser cutting and, if I cost it correctly, I may have to do only the assembling. I could even pay someone to help, or train a young person. At present my sister works with me, almost full-time when I'm busy and have the money. She's trained in fashion design and extremely dexterous; she's happier than I am to do the repetitive work, and she helps me with my books. With her, I've been learning how to delegate. I've realised that this is the way to handle larger orders if they come in. I used to worry in case they did! I'm not going to back away from them any more. If it means a decent income and time for designing, then it's worth doing it. It's not enough to moan endlessly about sore fingers and lack of money; after seven years it's cheating myself to think I'm doing well, when I'm not. It's time for some success.

Postscript: The American venture has proved successful with a large increase in production and turnover, and shorter delivery times. Use of laser cutting, together with batch production and outwork, has meant that I am able to handle the orders. I am confident that I can increase turnover further and I see profits and business opportunities resulting.

Jenni Hobbs

THE BITTER FRUIT OF SUCCESS
Creating a craft centre

Jenni Hobbs talked to Su Richardson about setting up a craft centre in the Midlands, a business venture she has entered into with her husband. Its growth and success have, ironically, led to alienation from her own craft. Her new organisational role works to the exclusion of her work in pottery, and she also finds herself labelled by the outside world as 'assistant' to her 'director' husband.

I was divorced and bringing up four children on my own, and decided I'd got to have a career, so I did a teaching degree with art as the main subject. At the end of my three-year course I got married again, acquired two extra children, making six altogether, and I took a part-time job teaching at an evening institute. The place I moved to with my husband had some outbuildings and we decided to turn them into a pottery for me. At that point my husband got involved in pottery as well. We both decided that we wanted to make pots, but I knew it would be difficult in our isolated situation. It would mean one of us would have to go out and sell the pots while the other stayed at home. The big red light started flashing and I realised we were going to get back into the rat race, the selling business my husband had been in before. The idea of a craft centre emerged because neither of us wanted to go back to that.

Our idea was that if you got several craftspeople together, you'd have more to attract the public to you. We planned a craft shop and a gallery with several craft activities going on. We were then offered a bigger property half a mile away in the village. There was lots of room for craftspeople to live and work, plus lots more exhibition space, and a place for a tea room. Help came from the Department of the Environment on certain parts of the property which are historic scheduled monuments, and the county council are utilising a manpower services community project to provide the labour.

But my potting has actually gone far, far into the background as the project has evolved. It is constantly put back, as other priorities take over.

There is a very creative side to organising and arranging exhibitions and meeting other craftspeople, but I miss losing myself in the physical work of my pottery. I refuse to dismiss my intended vocation as a potter. I've set myself up in a disused pantry and started already, although there isn't a kiln yet. In our previous place, Chris and I worked on everything together, and in a way I regret moving into this office role, typing and bookwork and general organisation, plus looking after the home. Chris is building mostly, and looking after the few animals we've got. Before, we did absolutely everything on a shared basis – floor laying, timber reclaiming, money earning, everything. That's completely changed now. I'm scared about slipping back into what appears to be an unequal relationship. It's more society that forces you into that feeling, because everyone assumes that Chris is the driving force, the master, the leading light; I'm just a secondary back-up facility, the domestic slave-cum-secretary. This is very bad for my self-image; it makes me angry and frustrated, so I come across as aggressive or petulant.

In my head I think that when I start potting properly, I shall be able to assert myself in an area of my own. At the moment we both see ourselves as potters. I taught Chris to throw, and he taught himself about kilns and he is excellent at it; already he is considered *the* potter. I don't know where that leaves me. It will be interesting to see over the next couple of years how things evolve and in what directions we go. I have often been tempted to change my craft and do something else, even though

ceramics are what I really want to do. I'm very interested in textiles, and he isn't, but it's terrible to think that I'm looking for something that he can't do. When one's reduced to that it's worrying. There must be equal numbers of women potters to men, but to hear the men talking about it you'd think it was all male. I feel that even if men aren't conscious of it, they do feel threatened by women coming into an equal working relationship. We need to find a realistic way of working through this and coping, otherwise promising relationships get destroyed.

I think I would feel a lot better if we weren't married. There is something about the wife tag that translates as appendage, assistant and what have you, and there is more to that than seems immediately obvious. For example, wives tend not to be in business partnerships with husbands because of the tax laws which take away vast allowances: I know lots of partnerships in reality, but the wife is claimed for as the secretary. To me it makes a big difference. I'm very conscious of our official relationship; however, I'm not prepared to do anything about that now. I have seen unmarried men and women working together and the man still attracts the response I've described. So marriage is only part of the problem.

I often feel I'd like to opt out of my situation and just work with women, but somehow I've got to find an answer to my problem here. This is the one bone of contention I have with some feminists, because although I know how good working with women can be, I don't think it is the only answer. We need to work out strategies to confront sexism in an

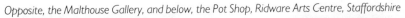

Opposite, the Malthouse Gallery, and below, the Pot Shop, Ridware Arts Centre, Staffordshire

unaggressive way, at the same time as constantly asserting ourselves. Sometimes it means that we are perceived as viragos; I find I often over-compensate and then people shrink away. But it's all possible on a one-to-one basis; something can be worked out between individual men and women. Many women don't fight the system in a large way; they accept a certain amount in order to carry on with what they want to do individually. This way they can achieve some personal success. So the choice is to work towards keeping your own sanity, self-image, and personality intact, or notching up a little bit for real change in a more public role. There is a problem of putting down the individual man all the time. That's no answer either – to be ruining a man's ego and undermining his self-confidence in an attempt to solve our own problems. But my husband has to take a lot of flak!

Lynn Ross

CO-OPERATIVE CRAFT ON ARRAN
Spinning, weaving and knitting

Co-operative working has been a feature of many
alternative enterprises in Britain since the late 1960s.
Lynn Ross describes one such venture on the island
of Arran, off the west coast of Scotland. Lynn points
to the central dilemma of the exercise as being
'how to produce the quality handcrafted item without
exploiting producer or consumer'. Lynn herself was
born in Scotland, though she lived much of her early
life in the United States and later in Sweden. It was in
Sweden, a country less scourged by industrialisation,
that Lynn was able to learn traditional methods of
spinning, weaving and dyeing.

Seven years ago I decided to return to Scotland from
Sweden and try to make a living from my weaving. In Sweden I'd been
teaching English and weaving part-time, managing to sell everything I could
make. I learnt spinning and dyeing so that I could make my own weaving
yarns, and reached the point where I wanted to make the practice of
these crafts a full-time occupation. So I went to Arran, though without
realising that these traditional household crafts had long ago been abandoned on the island, and that the 1960s 'back to nature' revival movement
hadn't happened here at all. There were only one or two weavers in a
place where every household once used to have a cottage loom.

One of the things that had attracted me to Arran was its form of
tourism, which suited the production and sale of crafts. The commercial
atmosphere, coupled with a beautiful location, made it seem a very
desirable place to set up a small business based on spinning, weaving and
dyeing, one that should be complementary to what was already going on.
Some years before I came, a craft co-operative had been set up on a
system of one person per craft, and one day per week active shop-keeping
and selling of each other's wares. At that time there was no spinner on
the island producing handspun yarn for sale, although there were one or
two weavers who had been trained in the Highlands. Natural dyeing

was something people vaguely remembered in connection with their grandmothers, a couple of generations ago. The crafts that were being produced were pottery, printmaking and jewellery, not particularly linked to the traditional island crafts associated with a crofting economy. Spinning and weaving as they had been practised before industrialisation in the west of Scotland had been virtually forgotten.

Before the farming 'reforms' which resulted in the clearances and the subsequent mass emigrations to Canada, farming was done on a communal basis and this included the processing of wool and flax. When the shearing was finished the women in the community would travel round the various farms with their spinning wheels, and work until all the spinning was done. There was great social importance attached to this time; when a young girl was getting married, for instance, the whole community would get together to card and spin the wool for her blankets. The family worked together too, in the production of textiles, with the children helping to clean and card the wool, the women spinning and the men weaving. The changes in farming methods and the emigration of families who had lost their land, along with the rapid rise of the textile industry on the west coast around Paisley and Ayrshire, meant inevitably that cheaper cloth was then imported from the mainland. The communal effort of production in the family and in the clachan, or village, became a thing of the past.

We try now to spin local fleece, although we have to be careful not to infringe the territory of the Wool Marketing Board. As things stand, the local farmer is supposed to send his fleece to the Wool Board and we are supposed to buy it back from the east coast of Scotland. A large proportion of the local fleece is from blackface sheep and no use for handspinning – its variation in staple length makes it difficult to spin a good quality, and the yarn tends to be coarse. But there are other breeds as well. Most of the local farmers have large enough flocks to be required by law to register with the Wool Board, but we are hoping that negotiation will make it possible for us to spin and sell local wool. This would at least save the freight to the mainland and back.

The other raw material of historical significance, which is now imported, is flax. In the early 1800s agricultural experts recommended the production of flax on Arran because of the climate and the availability of manure which would replenish the land after this scourging crop had been harvested each year. At one time linen thread spun from flax was the main export of the island, used for fishing nets. When the Scottish linen industry fell into decline with the advent of cotton, this source of income was lost as well. We have planted a trial crop this year and will spin the flax as a novelty yarn for weaving. In spite of the lapse of a century or so, the flowers seem to remember how to grow.

When I first started working on the island, I produced rag rugs and tapestries on an old loom which I had brought with me from Sweden. I set about adapting the techniques which I had learnt there to Arran's raw materials. For rugs and hangings I used a range of natural coloured fleeces complemented with dyes from local plants such as heather and birch leaves. Luckily many of the plants were the same as in Sweden, so it was possible to work out a range of vegetable dyes to be used on machine-spun wool which was already suited to the commercial patterns available at that time. The response in sales was encouraging enough in the first summer for me to want to continue another year. At the same time I made contact with an old man who had revived the wheelwright's trade on the island and was producing spinning wheels in traditional Scottish models. With my loom which I'd brought from Sweden, a locally made wheel and a few dye pots, I formally set up the Silverbirch Workshop in Whiting Bay.

Since the beginning there has been growth in many different directions and I like to think that the workshop has created an awareness of the potential of these crafts, and of their links with traditions as well. Although I had not intended to teach spinning and weaving, I found from the start that people asked if I would show them how, and gradually the workshop took on an educational side. At the local level it included demonstrations at meetings like the Women's Rural Institute, at the local museum and nature centre and in primary schools. For several years running I set up winter workshops to teach local women spinning and weaving, and from these have sprung different enterprises on the island. The two most significant are the Handspinners' Co-operative and the Knitters' Group.

Lynn Ross, a weaver from the Arran co-operative

P. C. JOWSEY

Each of these formed its own growth pattern, and has separated from the structure of the Silverbirch Workshop while still co-operating with it. There are, as well, a few handspinners who are not producing commercially but have pursued the craft to a level of excellence, which has won competitions such as the Royal Highland Show. Summer courses have been set up for visitors, and students have stayed here as part of their placement on degree courses.

THE HANDSPINNERS' CO-OP
At the same time as the winter workshops were under way, interest in handspun wool was growing and customer demand was steadily increasing. The summer orders to the Silverbirch Workshop were more than I could handle alone and it seemed a good idea to pass the orders on to the more experienced spinners in the workshops in order to meet the demand. By the following year, as competence and confidence increased, the idea developed that each spinner should produce her own designs for the summer season and that a co-operative be set up to market the yarns and garments produced. To me at that time this seemed ideal, because working on a co-operative basis appeared the best way for women and it would seem that I, too, would benefit from collective marketing. In the meantime I could get back to weaving, knowing that handspun wool would be available as well.

If at this stage we had appointed a co-op manager to co-ordinate our individual efforts, we might have had an easier time of setting up, but the main idea was to cut out any kind of middle person so that all the money would go directly to the spinner and to the co-op funds for advertising and so on. It was decided to set up a rota system of shopkeeping in our summer outlet (which for convenience's sake was the Silverbirch Workshop), with responsibility for book-keeping on a collective daily basis; we had an honorary secretary and treasurer.

The system failed. Everyone had a different level of commitment to the co-operative, and many had other considerations as well, such as hotels to run or small children to look after. As the spinning project was a supplementary income, it could never be given first priority. We did try to get outside assistance for funding, but were thwarted by details such as meetings with officialdom suggested for four o'clock in the afternoon just when all the children were coming home from school, or evening meetings in winter when public transport between villages is non-existent.

If we had been able to get funding at this stage each spinner would have been paid immediately she produced her wool, instead of having to finance her own effort on a sale or return basis. This is a concept not unprecedented in history. In the 1700s, when textile production was still a cottage industry, the British Linen Bank was set up in the west of Scotland to cover the cost of raw materials for the linen spinners and spun yarn for the weavers, until the production chain was complete. For us it proved difficult to get any funding because we could not guarantee production on any large scale. Ironically, we were turned down on one occasion because we had no power equipment – just at the time when the Harris weavers were being refused the Orb ('guaranteed hand-woven') mark if they motorised their looms. Generally, we were told that part-time employment for women was not a priority on the island, although we knew that money from the spinning project, in every case, was an important boost to the family economy.

Wool sales continued and wool orders came in to the Silverbirch Workshop at a good enough rate to encourage the group to work on at dealing with the problems. More applications for finance were turned down; in one case because we were apparently successful, and in another because we were a commercial operation. Finally we decided that the co-operative would function for the time being just to obtain raw materials in bulk at a cheap rate, still to be paid for by the spinners themselves. Instead of trying to run an outlet collectively, we settled on a compromise and worked through local shops which had the interest of good quality crafts at heart. We developed a small mail order system that reflected the individuality of each woman's work, because by now everyone was spinning quite differently and had developed her own style.

The group started with six members, swelled at one point to thirteen, and at present has four who feel that the concept of a co-operative is important enough to try and sort out the difficulties. Decision-making is easier and it is possible to establish a method of working which can grow from here.

Women from the Silverbirch workshop spin and sort wool outdoors

LYNN ROSS

THE KNITTERS' GROUP

The demand for garments was a natural development from spinning and led to the formation of a knitters' group, none of whom was particularly interested in learning to spin. Knitting is the one craft which has continued in this area, and the level of skill is extremely high as most girls are taught at an early age. But many of the techniques had been adapted to synthetic yarns and it was necessary to translate knitting into handspun terms. It was decided at an early stage that patterns for handspun should be very simple to allow the texture of the yarns to be shown to full advantage. This meant that the knitters had a quite straightforward task and could indeed work of an evening by the television. The knitters met in the beginning to determine their own fee, on a rate per ounce. As they were working primarily to order, the question of marketing didn't really arise, but it has always been the aim in both spinning and knitting to pay the women a minimum hourly wage for their work based on national wage scales. This makes the job quite well paid considering the conditions, and also means that the goods produced can be competitive for the customer. As with the yarns, it was decided with the garments to market directly and avoid large mark-ups from retail outlets. This has meant that effort has had to be put into a mail order structure, creating patterns for the yarns and sending out samples of the products. This year I have managed to present the whole project comprehensively in a mail order brochure, now that we know what is predictable and what can be reproduced.

We were fortunate in the knitters' group to have a woman whose father was a fisherman until the industry collapsed after the Second World War. She can still recall the designs that her mother used to knit into the pullovers for going to sea, and also what practical purpose each stitch had. These designs were very plain and did not follow the traditions of the Irish Aran Isles, although some of the motifs, like the cables, were the same. Again, for the knitters, the income is supplementary; most of them rely on other jobs as well, in local shops for example.

From the beginning, the two main criteria of design for handspun had to be simplicity and warmth, and because the main aim was commercial it had to be easy to produce the yarns and the garments in numbers without compromising quality. At the start, customers were drawn to the wool by its uniqueness and in many cases had their own ideas about what to do with it. But there were also people wanting to use the yarn who needed patterns for it, which is how the knitwear design section of the workshop began. I had not had experience in designing knitwear but I knew what I thought the yarns should look like knitted up, and it seemed best to start from first principles. We made garments based on classical shapes which would be warm without being too heavy and we let the texture of the wool speak for itself. We now have a range of basic yarns and shapes which seem to work best for handspun.

Our Handspinners' Co-operative had failed through lack of a manager.

But our co-operative *intentions* were to avoid the exploitation of women's skills, when a sweater costing a few pounds to make is retailed for hundreds at the other end of the marketing chain. (If we can't manage in the future to ensure that most of the money goes to the woman who produces the goods, then perhaps it is better that knitwear be made by machines.) Chronic lack of funding I now choose to see as having been an advantage. We have had to proceed slowly and at a pace that works for each woman's financial situation, and have thus avoided the tedium of eight-hour shifts. Future expansion should increase part-time work, rather than full-time. Such flexibility ensures that each woman has full control over her contribution and the development of her craft.

At several points during the development of this project, I have done consultative work for bodies concerned with setting up similar projects in third world developing countries. After I published a booklet explaining how to make patterns from handspun wool I received letters from all over the world, from government bodies and from individuals who were setting up spinning projects. Whether it was handspun mohair from Lesotho, or handspun, handknitted sweaters from Tristan da Cunha, the problems were identical to those encountered here. The issue was always: how does one produce a quality handcrafted item without exploiting producer or consumer? In the case of Arran, the handspinning wheel, a paradox in its own terms, is the most appropriate technology we can use. That we have no powered equipment is also a bonus in terms of maintenance; the machines can be repaired with a piece of string, a bit of wood or a hairpin if necessary.

With this technology and with designs that are simple to produce and that enhance the nature of the raw materials, it is possible for the spinners and knitters to provide a product which will pay them a decent wage and give the customer good value. If, in addition, we can use Scottish wool and flax with dyes off the hillside, then we are eliminating the crazy world-wide chain which results in Scottish people buying 'Shetland' sweaters made far from Scotland. If the result is to supply only our own small island with warm sweaters, then we shall have succeeded with our project. If we can market our work elsewhere and have the satisfaction of our skill being recognised as well, then we shall have succeeded with flying colours.

Looking back on the past seven years, I am very glad that I arrived when I did. It has meant that I could take part in these exciting developments, helping them grow and benefiting from them too. What knowledge there is of pre-industrial traditions on the island is being brought to the surface, to the consciousness of the people here, as the project gains credibility; local people are sharing their memories and family mementoes. Interestingly, a good deal of information can be gleaned from the areas in Quebec and New Brunswick where the Arran emigrants put down new roots, and where many of the old spinning and weaving designs can be found incorporated into the transatlantic traditions. Part of my work for the future will be to establish contact with spinners and weavers there, in order to find out more of the Arran traditions. I mean to apply the experiences and principles learnt from spinning and knitting to cloth-weaving; this could expand the possibilities of employment, and bring to light new historical connections.

Faith Gillespie

THE MASTERLESS WAY

Weaving an active resistance

Faith Gillespie, weaver, dyer and teacher of the crafts, celebrates craftwork as 'political dissent'. Since low-cost warehouse space on the Thames is no longer possible, as it has vanished into the hands of the property developers, her present weaving workshop is near London Bridge in a former garment factory, now a textile craft centre called Three Ply Craft.

They'd heard about me from someone, and came to see my work. Somehow they'd managed to find my workshop behind the high spiked iron gates in the seemingly derelict warehouse on the river in Wapping.

I just happened to have several finished orders not yet delivered, so there actually was something to show them. Most days there's really not a lot to see except a few samples of cloth, a shawl or two, and whatever is on the loom, because I work to commission: things are made and gone.

Well, *she*'d heard of me, and brought her husband trudging up the four flights of stairs and through the cavernous painting studios – she eager, he looking a bit nervous, both somewhat out of breath. A pleasant couple, midlife, prosperous (Jaeger, Aquascutum), they exclaimed at the splendid view of the Thames, asked me how I keep warm in winter (I don't: you can freeze meat here in January), admired the five-foot ashwood floorloom built for me by the woodworker Bruce Elton, and then turned their attention to the weaving.

She loved the tweed cloth, but he wasn't inclined to think of finding a tailor. They liked my flat-woven rugs and asked me how they could be hung on the wall. I said I make my rugs for bare feet but could show them how to mount one if they cared to. She touched everything, her fingers lingering longest over the tussah silk shawl.

In the end, they ordered a six-foot rainbow rug, and he wrote out a cheque to cover the cost of the materials. Then, as they were leaving, he looked around again and said, 'It must be nice to be able to make a living at your hobby.'

I don't have a hobby.

Craftsman Eric Gill said something like this: 'There are two kinds of people in the world – those who do what is required of them in their working time and do what they like to do in their spare time, and those who do what they like to do in their working time and do what is required of them in their spare time. The first are working for themselves and the second are working for God.'[1] I would say further that the first are working for themselves and the patriarchy. (Don't let's get stuck here in the problem about feminism and the patriarchal religions; see Mary Daly.[2] What is meant by the questionable word 'god' is, to me, that 'something in motion', within me and beyond me, towards which I move when I experience myself as maker.)

Of course you have a right to work for yourself (and/or the patriarchy), and I certainly have nothing against hobbies. After all, I teach people who want to weave for pleasure in their spare time. Making a well-woven object for yourself or someone else is very satisfying, and it can be a pacific, some say therapeutic, activity. But I'm not talking about those things. I'm talking about earning regular money from the craft – professionally – and that can scarcely be done, unless you are willing to put in the necessary twenty-seven hours a day, nine days a week, that the craft demands, and then do what is required in your spare time. You may have to be in love to do it: in love with the materials, the tools, the logic of the craft. The difference between a professional and an amateur is not that the amateur does it for love while the professional does it for money; no. Many professionals love their work, and an amateur may be paid. The real difference is that the professional does it whether she feels like it or not.

Given that a living does have to be earned, I am not yet convinced that earning a living is what life is about. But life *is* about work, about work and love. And economics, which is politics. And politics is about power. That is what I am talking about.

Born female into an entrenched social structure that is misplanned, misdirected, mismanaged and misogynist, we are constantly, from birth, both overpowered and underpowered. In a society which systematically exercises the power to say what we must be, what we must do, and what our value is, we labour under a lunatic economic construct that contaminates our minds, contaminates our lives. We are used and used, until we are used up, working for The Man and never paid enough.

We want something else, something entirely different.

In an article in *Craft* magazine some time ago, a writer was describing the personality traits that characterise the men (*sic*) who have kept the craft tradition alive and strong in Britain for centuries – self-reliance, pride of workmanship, wit, wisdom, and a finely turned leg (I can't remember the list) – and the key sentence was, 'The craftsman is the masterless man.' Well now, the answer to the plaintive query, 'What do women want?', is

ANNI SILVERLEAF

Faith Gillespie (left) and Jane Childs, weaving

perhaps too simple for obtuse minds, but it has been around for a long time: see Chaucer's Wife of Bath in *The Canterbury Tales*.

To be masterless: to be paid to do work that we like to do, that we can bring our own meanings to; to love in the ways that we like to love; to experience ourselves as the makers of our own lives. We resist the con of power as domination and control: I don't want to have a boss or be a boss. In making, we work in direct relationship to the power to *transform* – clay to bowl, molten glass to goblet, fibre to thread to cloth to cloak. Within the power to change raw materials by our hand into things both pleasing and useful lies an intimation of the possibility of transforming our lives. In this, we are sustained by a feeling of connected-ness and a sense of continuity, an awareness of our foremothers world-wide in a line that stretches back and back like a long warp into pre-history, to before our true powers were stolen, when women were the makers, making what was necessary: tools and spells, pots and baskets and blankets against the cold.

There is clearly another imperative at work now in our exercise of the old crafts. It has to do with reclamation, with reparation. The world seems not to need us any more to make 'the things of life'. Machines make more and cheap. The system needs us to do the maintenance jobs and to run the machines that produce the so-called 'goods', to *be* machines in the consumer societies which consume and consume and are empty. Our turning to craftwork is a refusal. We may not all see ourselves this way, but we are working from a position of dissent. And that is a political position.

Dissent costs.

When I delight in the witchery of the dyepot, turning heather into gold, I may not be risking the ducking pond, but I'm not making very much money. Dyeing wool with plants was once an ordinary household task, and housework (and all its extensions) is everywhere unpaid and underpaid.[3] While I'm stirring the pot and being masterless, happily in control of the means of production, I'm not securing index-linked pension funds or retirement benefits. There's no paid sick leave and no holiday, paid or otherwise. I never know where the next customer is coming from, or if anyone is coming at all. I weave fine craft things that are functional but not 'necessary' – one-off objects for a 'luxury market' – and I can't afford my own 'product'. I'm afraid, afraid that as the recession deepens, *no one* will be able to afford my work, and then what will I do? What if the 'phone is cut off? What will become of me when I'm old? What if the loom breaks down?

I get trapped in my thinking, and disturbed about the personal ambiguities and political contradictions inherent in making expensive rugs and silk scarves and alpaca shawls for the people with money, in a world where unemployment and inflation and anxiety and hunger are killing everyone else, a world of violence, destruction, wastefulness and greed. The tea's all gone and the rates bill's come and it's Friday and it's freezing and the Calor Gas bottle is about to run out and they won't bring another one till Tuesday and where will I find the £9 cash to pay for it (see Mrs Thatcher) and I must be out of my ever-lovin' cotton-pickin' blue-eyed brain to think that I can make a living making.

Contamination.

I should get a hobby. Something therapeutic.

I say I want to spin and dye and weave, to make useful things that I can sell. If the usual form of the livelihood question is 'How can I get enough money to live the way I want to?' I have to turn the question around and ask 'How can I live the way I want to on the least possible amount of money?' I can't think the word 'profit'. And from where I stand, 'security' is a word that costs more than I can afford. I want to live as a weaver.

So it's back to the loom. Back to Something in Motion, where my work is my inheritance, my pleasure, my occupation, my daily calling. All I have is time: time is the warp for the fabric of my life.

The theory, the politics, and the actualities of life form and inform one another, leading to action. If you want to learn to weave, you can buy a book and attempt to teach yourself: this can be a frustrating waste of time, even though the books are lovely.[4] You can enroll in a full-time college course, or go to art school, or do evening classes, or find someone to show you how. You need a little money and a loom of your own.

I wanted to be able to do it every day, as a regular practice, at home. I was sent to Lesley Millar, who is not only an excellent weaver but a very fine teacher as well. She advised me to start on a four-shaft tableloom, which doesn't cost an enormous amount, doesn't take up much space, and is easy to sell if you graduate to a bigger one, or if you find that it's not your path. When I stood at that little loom and began to weave, I felt I had been doing it for a thousand years or more. The knowledge seemed *found* in myself, recovered rather than acquired. And I knew that I could never learn it all, never use it up, never come to the end of it.

Lesley Millar was the perfect guide: she never told me too much too soon, she let me find out for myself. With the true teacher's gift for letting a process disclose itself, step by step, simply, she told me the ways of wool, how tension works, the precision the craft demands, the basic theory, methods and techniques, rules of cloth structure, principles of colour and design, the essential economy of time and materials, where and how to obtain equipment and supplies, how to plan and schedule the work, the importance of accurate record-keeping. She introduced me to tie-dyeing and to the amazement of indigo, and showed me how to mend a broken warp thread. 'There are no disasters in weaving,' she assured me. Years younger than me, skilful and thorough, she taught me the weaver's patience.

Then I came to Lynn Ross, way up on the Isle of Arran, off the west coast of Scotland. A most expert spinner, a dyer and knitter and weaver as well, she taught me spinning, the magical craft, showed me how the fleece and the wheel and the spinner form and inform each other. She initiated me into the practice of dyeing with plant stuffs gathered from the hillsides and marshes.

The first things I made were given away for birthday and Christmas presents. Gradually other people began to see my work and say, 'I like that, will you make one for me?' It was time to put a price on things. Coming to the limits of the tableloom, I moved to a bigger one. I needed more space and less isolation. Through a friend, I got a little workshop in the warehouses in Butler's Wharf, near Tower Bridge, where there were more than a hundred artists and craftworkers, and the rent was £1 a week. I gave up my freelance editing job, and there I was: a weaver. There were times I did other jobs to get by – many of us need to do that, anything from teaching (which can be an extension of your own work) to working in a pub (which you do in your spare time), but for the most part, I live by the loom.

The three questions people ask me most often are 'How much does it cost?' (the scarf or mat or whatever), 'How long does it take you to weave it?' and 'Where do you find your market?' Crucial questions, ones I often ask myself. They are raised frequently in articles in the guild journals and craft magazines. They are a prime subject of conversation whenever makers meet.

We all struggle with the problem of pricing our work. Time and money, money and time. 'Exchange value' and 'what the market will bear'. Some years ago, I met a woman at a craft fair who was selling nicely woven placemats, a set of six for £10, and quite attractive ponchos for £17, and I said to her, 'How can you do it? I can scarcely buy the materials for that price.' 'Well,' she said, 'my husband's a dentist, and I just need to pay for the yarn.' 'You're making it tough for the rest of us,' I said.

No one goes into craftwork for the purpose of getting rich, but in the crafts known traditionally as 'women's work', we face a particular difficulty: Womantime, especially when we stay in our 'place', is not taken to be worth very much. We may choose to give it away if we like, but it's all we have, and we need to be acutely aware of its importance. It's not that 'amateurs are ruining the business', but that we have to stop thinking that we don't deserve much, stop discounting ourselves. We owe to ourselves and to one another a rigorous practical assessment of the real value of our life time and our skills, refusing to allow what we do to be undervalued, devalued, exploited any more. As pedlars, wherever we find our market – craft shop or stall, gallery or private exhibition, through small adverts or word of mouth – we need more than the maker's patience, we need a fair price. It's about time.

The questions are difficult, the issues complex, the solutions situational and personal; this is not, however, an individualistic politic. Dissent is not a private matter, and the 'personal solution' is not enough. We are not doing 'private enterprise', we are not in the 'craft business'. The masterless way is a way of active resistance. We are workers living in public protest.

The circumstances of the times are shifting. Although money is getting tighter and tighter, more and more people are becoming aware of and interested in buying fine craftwork, or wanting to become craftworkers. There is a new 'craft movement' afoot, something growing that may bloom the way the white yarn from the indigo vat turns blue when it hits the air. There is something-in-motion. We, the makers, have at hand a glowing opportunity to establish ourselves in a new kind of marketplace which we are helping to define as it develops. As in all making, we will see what it looks like as it emerges.

It is not a 'competitive market' – what we do has nothing to do with competition. We do not make alike, and we can't make many. Indeed, we are forming a very real web of co-operation, both visible and invisible. It has little to do with 'design for industry', turning out 'mass market commodities'. We are working to our own design, making what is wanted and needed at quite another level of human life, meeting needs less tangible, needs as real as rainbows.

In talking about all these things today with my good weaver friend Jo Llewellyn, we agreed that the time is now. 'What we make is good and will last,' she said, 'and we must hold on to our belief in what we are doing.'

Those who want what we make are by no means only the 'people with money'. In addition to the 'prosperous', they are young couples in their first flat, an actress working on the fringe or out of work and living on the dole, a student supporting herself as a daily, a restaurant cook with two kids, a speech therapist, a widow and pensioner, clerical workers and shop assistants, artists teaching part-time, other craftworkers – all these people who have commissioned me to make something for them have one thing in common: they are refusing the more and cheap. They want something that speaks to them, something beautiful in their daily lives. Sometimes they pay over several months, and that's all right. Sometimes we trade – the man who painted my ceiling has a rug in exchange. I have a coffee mug made by a fine potter friend twenty years ago, and every morning when I use it, the hand of the maker is there. What I paid him for it was a loaf of homemade bread.

In keeping the crafts alive, we are keeping ourselves alive and keeping dissent alive. But that's not only what it is about. We could make our living in other ways and still do what we like to do in our working time. And dissent against the dehumanising patriarchal forces of control and domination is everywhere. It finds many forms, some difficult, even dangerous, as in the continuing action at Greenham Common; some as intuitive as the return to the herbal remedies and healing hands of 'complementary medicine'; some simple, like buying free-range eggs. It all makes a difference.

But I am talking about reclamation, reparation, and the power of women. And about record-keeping. Historically. Which is political.

Once there was a time when everything made was craft. The word itself used to mean 'strength, power, force'. And 'magic'. Further back than we can know, before the Maker-god was called 'Father', in the time when there were no masters, the power of making was ours. In the time before Mantime, our mysteries were interwoven with the lives of other women. We didn't write books, we *told* our craft. The power that is knowledge was ours, and given to our daughters and their daughters. Now we are left with the labour, but our power is broken and scattered.

We come to understand the importance of accurate record-keeping as we realize how our ancient and continuous history has been suppressed, how the work of the lives of uncountable unnamed women forever has been purposefully hidden, buried, denied, obliterated. Systematically. The woman who sat in the parlour and embroidered, the woman who sat in the chimney corner spinning for her family, the woman who wove the linens for the gentry and had no bedsheet for herself, the Bengali woman sewing piecework in East London, whatever else may be said, were all equally mastered and equally effaced, unrecorded, their lives made and gone. Judy Chicago says, 'All the institutions of our culture tell us – through words, deeds, and even worse, silence, that we are insignificant. But our heritage is our power; we can know ourselves and our capacities by seeing that other women have been strong.'[6]

In keeping faith with the age-old crafts, we bring a recognition, a validation of all the making women who came before us. By the work of our hand we celebrate them and ourselves, as far back as we can imagine and till now.

Among the Navajo people, one of the last matrilineal cultures to survive in the West, the weaver was held in highest esteem. In a Navajo burial place has been found the mummy of a weaver, wrapped in a blanket woven of the breast feathers of the golden eagle and sheets of spun cotton. Along with bowls of food and tools of the craft, she was buried with three miles of thread.

That three miles of thread knows no limits, it alters time and bends space, stretching back and back to all places.

We are mending the warp thread.

AFTERWORD

'Machines make more and cheap.' Producing hand-made or individually crafted items in a world overwhelmed by mass-produced and cheap goods seems anachronistic. The time it takes to make handcrafted items means that their prices are comparatively high, and often an item which falls into the luxury class brings scant profit to the craftswoman who made it ('I can't afford my own product'). Given in addition the sliding scale of values for craft and art, the closer craft gets to art status, and therefore the further away from an equivalence in mass production, the higher the price. This has already happened, as their titles denote, for 'artist potters' and 'fibre artists', for example. Art values are also to some extent relied on by the craftworker in her assumption of her product's superiority over the merely machine-made. Just as the notion that there is value in the visible 'mark' of the artist shows in the divergence of pricing between the print and the painting, so the same notion surfaces in the pricing of craft. As a consequence, the craft product may be sold only to those who are wealthy, as is art. Very high pricing draws attention to the cultural qualities of the craft; it may often express a desire for acceptance from the dominant culture. The artefact will then be called 'art', the craft roots minimised and 'needs as real as rainbows' dismissed.

Accepting cash payment for craftwork learnt as part of family tradition ('by my craftwork I am inextricably bound to my grandmother'), as a hobby ('the favoured would receive a home-made present'), or even out of domestic necessity ('although we respect the skills passed on to us, they stink of poverty'), means leaving a private world and becoming visible outside ('here's my heart, here's my soul'). Being accountable on the marketplace for crafts which are part of a domestic tradition expressing care and love ('recognising pieces of my father's trousers, her old coats') is frequently experienced as pain. Market relations are no substitute for human relations. Similarly, the pleasure in the making of the craft is reduced after the product has acquired a price. Sometimes this is unbearable, as in the case of a woman we know who knits cashmere garments for a craft shop, and for which she will accept no payment; she subverts the system, but only at personal financial cost. Given the market relations of our society, many women under-price their work because, actually, no price seems suitable. Covering the cost of materials provides the excuse for continuing a pleasurable activity. ('All my earnings do for me is enable me to carry on buying the materials'). That way, the time can still be given in love, our caring needs satisfied, and total alienation refused. 'Dissent costs.'

It can be politically appropriate for women craftworkers to own their means of production, if only a needle, to avoid the meaningless tasks of alienated wage labour. Outside the domestic situation, work is now less often within the mental control of the worker. This has been one result of the de-skilling process, and it has made us value what we know as 'creative' work as opposed to any other kind. It is this control that our contributors relish, despite their low income. A recent survey conducted by the Crafts Council showed that more women than men worked in the crafts, but that economically they fared far worse[1] ('I was actually living on part-time adult education teaching'). Fewer women are able to work full-time ('it was making art out of bits and pieces in between the nappies and the washing-up') and fewer have a specific space to do so ('I was alone at home, with the baby, working in a corner of the bedroom every day'). The Crafts Council findings, borne out by our contributors' comments, reflect the material conditions of women at home, surrounded by other duties and with few resources. Even at the end of the craft spectrum occupied by homeworkers, desire for increased control over their lives has affected the decision to work at home. Here, in addition there are strong economic pressures: 'without it you couldn't survive'. Myth states that woman's work is to supplement the family income, that earned by the male. The reality is that a third of family units no longer have a male at all, and many of the rest have only an unemployed one. The socialisation of men carries with it notions of the dignity of labour, providing a motivation to unionisation. The socialisation of women has given dignity with our caring roles, isolated within the nuclear family. This is a major reason why we accept low pay in homeworking, and why we under-price on the market ('it's difficult to think of charging much for it') because it doesn't seem to affect our dignity. But 'we need a fair price.'

These then are the dilemmas. Women's traditions seem tenuous. Our crafts have survived through being transformed and put under the male order, so misrepresented as art; alternatively they exist unofficially and without sanctions or value. The female values of co-operative caring do not sit happily with male individualising, and essentially competitive imperatives to self-fulfilment. These last are the imperatives that determine the dominant culture. But craftwork could give us the opportunity to intervene in male cultural relations without losing our 'other' value system, including those values, for example, 'which have been missing from the cultural scene – caring, modesty, gentleness'. Our unofficial traditions are not tenuous; they merely seem so, being private. Our interventions could be a coming out, to each other, the personal being political. We can aspire to self-determination, not as individuals with a special craft interest, but as a community of women both creating and consuming our crafts. Consumption is crucial and is not just about buying and using because usage provides us with experience of the craft and through that experience we may participate to create a dynamic of cultural engagement.

Craft is common. It is common in having low status. It is common as something in which so many of us participate. Our crafts are common in being unsanctioned; they have not been much raked for the production of 'genius', they remain our property and embody our domestic values.

Our common feminine traditions are expressed in our craftwork, and as a community of women we can find self-determination in the commonality of our crafts by creatively making and consuming. Our co-operative, caring roles in the family, the values that dignify us there, deserve celebration through our cultural engagement.

USEFUL INFORMATION

CRAFTS COUNCIL, 12 Waterloo Place, London SW1Y 4AU.
For general information grants and loans; selected index of craftspeople and general register of craftspeople; also books and slide packs.

ADVICE AND POSSIBLE FINANCE
Council for Small Industries in Rural Areas (CoSIRA), 141 Castle Street, Salisbury, Wiltshire SP1 3TB.
Small Firms Division, Department of Industry, Abell House, John Islip Street, London SW1P 4LN.
Practical Action, 1 Hanway Place, London W1P 9DF: appeals for trust money for the young unemployed.
The Royal Jubilee Trusts, 8 Buckingham Street, London WC2 OBU: help given to young people.
Barrow and Geraldine Cadbury Trust, 2 College Walk, Selly Oak, Birmingham B29 6LE.
Registrar of Friendly Societies, 17 Audley Street, London W1X 2AP.
London Enterprise Agency, 69 Cannon Street, London EC4: help with money problems – free service.
Action Resource Centres at 9 Henrietta Place, London W1; 201 Upper Street, Islington, London N1; 1 Curzon Street, Birmingham 4; 54 Shadwick Place, Edinburgh: help with business problems – free service.
Project Fullemploy Resource Bank, 120 Clerkenwell Workshops, 31 Clerkenwell Close, London EC1: information and advice for people setting up a business – free service.
The National Federation of Self-Employment and Small Businesses, 32 St Anne's Road West, St Anne's, Lancashire.
Alliance of Small Firms and Self-Employed People, 279 Church Road, London SE1.
Regional Arts Associations – look in your local telephone directory.

Scotland only
Scottish Development Agency, Small Business Division, 102 Telford Road, Edinburgh EH4 2NT.

Wales only
Welsh Development Agency, Small Business Unit, Box 6, Ladywell House, Park Street, Newtown, Powys SY16 1JB.
Welsh Arts Council, Craft Department, Holst House, 9 Museum Place, Cardiff, South Wales.

Co-operative funding and advice
Co-operative Development Agency, 20 Albert Embankment, London
   SE1 7TJ.
Industrial Common Ownership Movement Ltd., Beechwood College,
   Elemete Lane, Roundhay, Leeds L88 2LG.
Co-operative Productive Federation, 30 Wandsworth Bridge Road,
   London SW6.
Job Ownership Ltd., 42-44 Hanway Street, London W1P 9DE.

Organisations
Equal Opportunities Commission (EOC), Overseas House, Quay
   Street, Manchester 3; also offices in Northern Ireland, Scotland
   and Wales.
The Association of Weavers, Spinners and Dyers, the Lace Guild, the
   Quilters Guild and the Knitting and Crochet Guild can all be
   contacted through The British Crafts Centre, 43 Earlham Street,
   London WC2H 9LD.
Federation of Women's Institutes of England and Wales, 39 Ecclestone
   Street, London SW1: publications and information concerning WI
   markets.
Women and Manual Trades, Unit V, 25 Horsell Road, London N5.

COLLECTIONS
Victoria and Albert Museum, South Kensington, London SW1.
Gawthorpe Hall, Padiham, Burnley, Lancashire.
Crafts Study Centre, Holburne Museum, University of Bath, Great
   Pulteney Street, Bath BA2 4DB.
It is necessary to make an appointment to see textiles from the
   collections as most of them are not on display.

RESEARCH
Feminist Library, Hungerford House, Victoria Embankment, London
   WC2.
Women Artists' Slide Library, Fulham Palace, Bishop's Avenue, London
   SW6.

NOTES

Part One

Housewives, Leisure Crafts and Ideology
1 Broughton, E. 'Home Economics', *Design Education in Schools*, ed. Aylward, B. Evans, London, 1973, p. 98.

Part Two

Sewing as a Woman's Art
1 Quoted from Gottesman, p. 276, in Orlofsky, Patsy and Myron, *Quilts in America*, McGraw Hill, NY, 1974, p. 26.
2 Interview with Mrs Snaith of Northumberland in 1978, courtesy of the Shipley Art Gallery, Gateshead.
3 See, for example, Jonathan Holstein, Foreword to *American Quilts*, catalogue of the National Museum of Modern Art, Kyoto, 1976.
4 Quoted in P. Cooper and N. B. Buferd, *The Quilters*, Audio Press, Bognor Regis, 1978, p. 75.
5 Interview with Mrs Little in 1978, courtesy of the Shipley Art Gallery, Gateshead.
6 W. Kandinsky, 'Reminiscences,' in *Modern Artists on Art*, ed. Robert Herbert, Prentice Hall, New Jersey, 1964, provides a classic example of the emphasis on individual expression.
7 H. White and C. White, *Canvases and Careers*, Wiley, Chichester, 1965, an account of the presentation of the Impressionists' work to the public, describes how a clearly recognisable individuality became the basis of an artist's saleroom identity.
8 Interview with Mrs Little, op.cit.
9 Quoted in P. Cooper and N. B. Buferd, op. cit., p. 76.
10 Mavis FitzRandolph, *Traditional Quilting*, Batsford, London, 1954, p.151.
11 Quoted in P. Cooper and N. B. Buferd, op. cit., p. 143.

Craft as Art
1 Florence Nightingale, *Cassandra*, 1852, quoted by R. Bridenthal and C. Koonz, eds., *Becoming Visible: Women in European History*, Houghton Mifflin & Co., Boston, 1979, p. 315.
2 See Carl Gustave Jung, *Man and his Symbols*, Aldus Books, London, 1964, p. 60.
3 These ideas were originally discussed during a seminar series 'On Reading' held by Sarat Maharaj at Goldsmith's College, London in 1980.

4 Claude Levi-Strauss, *Structural Anthropology*, Allen Lane, London, 1968, pp. 251-6.
5 This idea originates from Jacques Lacan and was discussed as part of the above seminar series.
6 Mary Daly, *Gyn/Ecology: The Metaethics of Radical Feminism*, Women's Press, London, 1979, pp. 77, 78.
7 'Animus' refers to the essence of man within woman: it is also defined as 'life force' and 'animating spirit', 'soul' or 'mind'. Conversely, 'anima' is the essence of woman within man.

Potters of the 1920s
1 See Anthea Callen, *Women in the Arts and Crafts Movement 1870-1914*, Astragal Books, London, 1979.
2 Most of the following quotations are taken from reviews in *The Times* during the 1920s. The main reviewer was Charles Marriott, whose treatment of the crafts was serious and informed. It was of enormous benefit to craftspeople and galleries alike and helped to promote a sympathetic audience for craft exhibitions in London. Muriel Rose, who ran the Little Gallery, remembers how helpful were his reviews as publicity for the exhibitions.
3 J. V. G. Mallet, introduction to reprint of *The Cheyne Book of Chelsea Potters*, 1973.
4 It is very difficult to find information about these women, but all the following exhibited their work in London in the 1920s: Dorothy Bell, Irene M. Browne, Stella Crofts, Sybil Finnimore, Irene Cooke, Lily Norton, Constance Stella Watson, Jessamine Bray, Joan West, Aline Ellis, Miss Sleigh and Miss Simpson.

Part Three

The Wider Last of Shoemaking
1 The Industrial Common Ownership Movement gave the women a grant in 1972. For further details, see Judy Wajcman, *Women in Control*, Open University Press, Milton Keynes, 1983.
2 *Shoe and Leather News*, March 1983, p. 6.
3 Ibid.
4 *Shoe Show* catalogue, ed. K. and K. Baynes, Crafts Council, London, 1979, p. 13.
5 David and Inger Rink, *Shoes for Free People*, Unity Press, Santa Cruz, California, 1976.
6 See *Hayward Gallery* annual catalogue, Arts Council, London, 1978, p. 41.
7 W. A. Rossi, *Sex Life of the Foot and Shoe*, Routledge & Kegan Paul, London, 1977, pp. 67-8.

8 She talks about her work in the *Shoe Show* catalogue, op. cit., pp. 77-9.

Hidden Worlds

1 Over 60 per cent of firms employ less than 20 workers (these figures are based on 1977 statistics, the latest available, and are cited in *From Rags to Rags: Low Pay in the Clothing Industry*, by Simon Crine and Clive Playford, Low Pay Unit, 1982).
2 London Borough of Camden Employment Committee, 4 July 1983, Agenda Item No. 5.
3 In 1981, homeworkers' average hourly wage taken from the Leicester Outworkers' Campaign Survey was 75p. Out of the 50 homeworkers interviewed in the survey 70 per cent (35 women) earned less than £1 an hour and of those 12 earned less than 50p. See *Homeworking Campaigns: Dilemmas and Possibilities in Working with a Fragmented Community*, Mary Hopkins, Leicester Outwork Campaign. In the Low Pay Unit Survey on Homework, 1984, hourly rates ranged from 7p to £4 an hour. A third of traditional homeworkers earned 50p an hour or less and just over three-quarters earned £1 or less. See *Sweated Labour: Homeworking in Britain Today*, Liz Bisset and Ursula Huws, Low Pay Unit, 1984. The Wages Council minimum hourly rate of pay for women workers in the clothing industry is £1.88 per hour (1987 figures). The majority of homemakers are paid well below this, earning often as little as 50p an hour.
4 North East London Polytechnic.
5 Greenwich Homeworker Project, Annual Report, 1985, p.5.

Artist Craftswomen between the Wars

1 Correspondence between Phyllis Barron and Muriel Rose, 1934-38; letter from Barron to Rose from this period dated 7 October.
2 Phyllis Barron and Dorothy Larcher Order Book, April 1938-December 1945.
3 Heather Tanner, *Biography of Phyllis Barron*, largely compiled from the recording of a talk given by Phyllis Barron at Dartington Hall, Dartington, in 1964.
4 Ella McLeod, 'Elizabeth Peacock, 1880-1969', monograph, *Weaving by Elizabeth Peacock*, Crafts Study Centre exhibition catalogue, Bath, 1978.
5 See note 3.
6 See note 4.
7 Catalogue for the First Exhibition of Spinning, Weaving and Dyeing organised by the GWSAD, Whitechapel Art Gallery, 1935.
8 Barley Roscoe, 'Flax and Fleece', *Crafts*, 45, July-August 1980.

Documentation on the craftswomen mentioned, together with all docu-
ments listed here, are held in the Crafts Study Centre, Holburne Museum
(University of Bath). A Weaver's Life: Ethel Mairet (1852-1972) by Margot
Coatts, published by the Crafts Council, 1983, gives the definitive account
of her life and work.

Embroiderers at Home
 1 Textile Aspects – Sixty-Two Group, September 1982, exhibition catalogue.
 2 Unpublished paper by Karen Harrison, 'Contemporary Embroiderers'.

The Masterless Way
 1 See Eric Gill, Art, Nonsense and other Essays, Cassell, London, 1929.
   The person who actually said it was Ananda Coomaraswamy, first
   husband of Ethel Mairet, friends of Eric Gill. Or maybe Ethel Mairet
   said it.
 2 Mary Daly, Beyond God the Father: Towards a Philosophy of Women's
   Liberation, Beacon Press, Northampton, 1973.
 3 See Selma James and Mariarosa Della Costa, The Power of Women and
   the Subversion of the Community, Falling Wall Press, Bristol, 1972.
 4 See Rachel Brown, New Key to Weaving, Macmillan, London, 1976;
   Mary E. Black, The Weaving, Spinning and Dyeing Book, Routledge &
   Kegan Paul, London, 1978; Peter Collingwood, The Techniques of Rug
   Weaving, Faber & Faber, London, 1968; Marianne Straub, Handweaving
   and Cloth Design, Pelham Books, London, 1977.
 5 If you want to investigate the subject for yourself, I recommend the
   section called 'Making a Living At It' in Rachel Brown's The Weaving,
   Spinning and Dyeing Book, with its introduction by Edith Farmer; see
   note 4. The approach is comprehensive and realistic, the information
   valuable.
 6 Judy Chicago, The Dinner Party: A Symbol of Our Heritage, Anchor
   Press/Doubleday, Bognor Regis, 1979.

Conclusion
 1 Alex Bruce and Paul Filner, Working in Craft: An Independent Socio-
   economic Study of Craftsmen and Women in England and Wales, Crafts
   Council, London, 1983.